TAROT
WORKBOOK

Featuring the classic Sharman-Caselli deck

Juliet Sharman-Burke

CONNECTIONS
BOOK PUBLISHING

To Jess, with love

A CONNECTIONS EDITION
This edition published in Great Britain in 2004 by
Connections Book Publishing Limited
St Chad's House, 148 King's Cross Road
London WC1X 9DH
www.connections-publishing.com

British Library Cataloguing-in-Publication data available on request.

ISBN 1-85906-143-5

1 3 5 7 9 10 8 6 4 2

Phototypeset in Cochin using QuarkXPress on Apple Macintosh
Origination by Bright Arts, Singapore
Printed by Donnelley Bright Sun, China

CONTENTS

INTRODUCTION

The Deck

The Sharman-Caselli deck was born when I was asked to create a new yet traditional tarot. My aim was to produce a deck with clear symbolism that would be both close to the spirit of the early decks yet continue to be relevant in the modern world. The Minor Arcana was inspired by the Waite deck, created in 1910 by occultist Arthur Waite and artist Pamela Colman-Smith, which uses full pictorial imagery on each of the Minor Arcana cards. However, the Major Arcana in the Waite deck deviates considerably from the early decks, both in imagery and numbering (the Major Arcana cards of the earliest decks had no names or numbers). The Major Arcana in the Sharman-Caselli deck takes its inspiration and influence from the imagery found on older decks such as the fifteenth-century Visconti Tarot and eighteenth-century Tarot de Marseilles.

The colour schemes for the Minor Arcana cards were specially chosen to reflect the element of each suit. Red, yellow and orange are used as key colours for the fiery suit of Wands; soft blue and pink for the watery suit of Cups; ice blue, mauve and grey for the airy Swords; and brown and green for the earthy Pentacles. The Major Arcana uses traditional colour associations, such as red for passion, white for purity and purple for wisdom, to expand each card's symbolic significance. The full Sharman-Caselli deck is featured in colour, for your reference, on the front and back flaps of the book. This workbook presents you with the opportunity to create your own personal colour scheme for the deck (more about this opposite).

The Students

The imagery of each card is fully explained in the book-and-cards package *Beginner's Guide to Tarot*. In this workbook my task is to help you understand the cards in a deeper, more personal way. With this in mind, I was kindly given permission to record the experiences and insights of a small group of students who studied with me intensely. It was a great privilege to work with such a wonderfully diverse group over a period of several months. Their mix of ages, backgrounds and life experiences produced a wide range of associations to the cards.

As you read each student's personal account of their understanding of the cards, I hope their connections and opinions will stimulate your own ideas. My intention is for you to feel as much a part of a student group as possible so you can start to form your own 'association bank'. I hope these insights will be useful for you to draw on when doing readings, both for yourself and others. You might even like to form your own tarot group to discuss ideas, impressions and opinions about the imagery with others.

The Card Exercises

Reading the tarot sensitively requires a well-developed imagination and sense of intuition. With this aim in mind, you are strongly encouraged to complete the exercises that appear with each card. These have been designed to help you form a close relationship with each image and to organize your study of the tarot effectively.

The 'Personal association' exercise encourages you to relate the meanings of each card to your own experiences. Compare or contrast your associations with those of the students. Use the section 'What this image means in my life' to record impressions which may have been stimulated by reading the student comments.

Colouring in the archetypal images will stimulate your imagination unconsciously. As the divinatory meanings start to unfold automatically, the images will soon start to feel like old friends. We all have our own ideas about colour and its meaning, so the colouring exercise offers you an opportunity to design your own scheme. While experimenting with coloured pencils or paints, you will find that you are connecting with the images in a less intellectual, more intuitive fashion, which is the approach you need to unlock the secrets of the tarot. (NOTE: if using paints, you may find it easier to work on photocopies of the card images.)

While the Sharman-Caselli deck uses pastel colours, you may prefer something stronger; or you may decide on different colour associations for the four elements. This is your chance to experiment in whatever way you choose. As the tarot works on many levels, there are various ways to approach it: emotionally, intuitively, intellectually and pragmatically. These in turn correspond to the four elements – water, fire, air and earth – and the Jungian four functions of consciousness: feeling, intuition, thinking and sensation.

The Minor Arcana and
the Four Elements

The Minor Arcana is made up of fifty-six cards divided into four suits – Cups, Wands, Swords and Pentacles – and this is where we shall begin. The suits each contain cards numbered from Ace to Ten, plus four court cards: Page, Knight, Queen and King. Each suit describes experiences relating to a sphere of life: the suit of Cups connects with the element of water and the realm of feeling; Wands connects with the element of fire and the realm of imagination; Swords connects with the element of air and the realm of thinking; while the suit of Pentacles connects with the element of earth and the material realm.

In this workbook, I have grouped cards of the same number together. This is to help you get a real sense of how the energy of the element works through the numbers in the four suits. We will discuss all the Aces together, then the Twos, Threes, and so on. It will soon become clear that, while the numbers preserve their individual meanings, their relevance is influenced according to the elements in which they are placed. For example, the Aces, which signify beginnings, reveal a different kind of new start in the feeling-oriented Cups than in, say, the fiery Wands or practical Pentacles.

As you work through each set of numbers, you will start to develop an intuitive understanding of both the numbers and the elements. This will make interpreting readings much easier and it will become a more natural process.

The Numbers

ACE: Ace is the number One, signifying creative power and potential. It symbolizes all beginnings, with the attendant upsurge of energy, and is the number from which all the other numbers grow.

TWO: The pure energy of the Ace is divided into opposing forces which may conflict or balance. The number Two reveals opposites such as positive and negative, male and female, spirit and matter.

THREE: Three is the number of growth, expansion and initial completion. One contains the idea, Two is the pair that can carry out the idea and Three is the fruit of the partnership.

FOUR: Four is the number of reality, logic and reason. The essence of man's three-fold nature of body, mind and spirit is brought to the material plane when it forms a square.

FIVE: Five is the number of uncertainty. When another dimension is added to the solid Four, the energy is disrupted, so the vibration of the Five constantly shifts and changes.

SIX: Six is the number of harmony and equilibrium. The six-pointed star is created out of two triangles, one pointing up towards the heavens or spirit, while the other points down towards the earth or the body.

SEVEN: Seven is the number relating to wisdom and knowledge. Following the peaceful balance of the Six, Seven represents serious choices and changes but, as it is a profound number, the changes usually come from the inner rather than the outer world.

EIGHT: Eight is the number of death and regeneration. After death, a new life begins, so baptismal fonts generally have eight sides.

NINE: The energies of all the other numbers gather together in Nine to form a foundation before completion can take place.

TEN: Ten is perfection through completion. The One of beginning is placed next to the Zero of spirit so the cycle is complete.

The Court Cards

The court cards are treated as a separate group, with the Pages, Knights, Queens and Kings also grouped in fours. We will look at the astrological links between the court cards, noting that the elements and their astrological qualities of cardinal, fixed and mutable correspond with the King, Queen and Knight respectively. The cardinal energy of the Kings initiates action, the fixed energy of the Queens preserves and contains action, while the mutable energy of the Knights changes action, and the Pages act as a reflection of each element's essence.

The Major Arcana

We will then turn our attention to the twenty-two cards of the Major Arcana, looking closely at the important symbolism and deeper meaning of each card. The Major Arcana cards represent stages in an individual's life cycle rather than specific events, which are more easily connected with the Minor Arcana. The first card, The Fool, represents the start of a new phase in life. If we were looking at chronological life, this card would represent birth. However, as the cycles of life keep repeating, and each has a beginning, a middle and an end, so The Fool is a symbol of all beginnings while The World symbolizes all their completions.

ACE *of* CUPS

The Ace of Cups reflects emotions overflowing. Five streams of water – representing the five senses – pour over the rim of the jewelled cup. The cup is made of gold, a valuable metal that corresponds to the preciousness of feelings. The abundance of water overflowing into the pool below is an image of an outpouring of emotion.

ACE *of* CUPS

Within a reading

All the Aces represent the start of something new. In the suit of Cups, which symbolizes feelings, the Ace reveals a powerful beginning in the area of emotions. This may be around relationships, falling in love or connecting deeply with another person on an emotional level.

Student comments

CARA (24) *The Ace of Cups makes me think of the beginning of my first big relationship, the first time I had ever really fallen in love. It was a fantastically intense feeling. I felt completely overwhelmed by tender emotions whenever I was with the man I loved. I remember being amazed that any ordinary thing suddenly looked extraordinary when I was with him; a pleasant sunny day would seem simply wonderful whenever I was with him.*

Cara's response is a typical one for the Ace of Cups, as she describes the passion and outpouring of feelings so often experienced in the early stages of a love affair.

GERALDINE (62) *This card makes me think of the first time I held my little grandson in my arms. I fell deeply in love with him from that moment. I clearly remember being filled with the most incredible sense of awe and tenderness. I don't remember experiencing quite such intensity when my own daughter was born, yet my grandson's birth made me aware of a profound sense of joy and wonder in the miracle of life.*

The Ace of Cups represents that special moment when one's normal way of feeling is heightened and concentrated. It cannot last, simply because we could not function indefinitely experiencing such emotional intensity, but while it does, it represents an emotional encounter likely to have a profound effect on our psyche.

NAME

DATE

PLACE

TIME

Colouring exercise
As you colour in this image, choose colours that remind you of emotional experiences. The important thing to remember is that you are trying to imbue the image with something from your emotional world.

Personal association
Think about all the different times in your life to which this image could be relevant. Record as many as you can, comparing and contrasting the intense feelings of love or hate that a certain event or relationship evoked.

What this image means in my life _____

_____

_____

_____

Readings in which it was significant _____

_____

_____

_____

See Reading Record Sheet of _____

ACE *of* WANDS

The fiery suit of Wands finds its Ace signifying a new start in the area of creativity and imagination. The number One stands for beginnings and Wands is the suit of visions, so when the two combine they reflect the energy and excitement present at the moment when a new idea is conceived. The single wand symbolizes an idea which apparently comes from nowhere (the clouds), while the distant castle represents the actualization of a dream or vision.

ACE *of* WANDS

to a friend about nothing much when an idea began to form in my head based on a previous experience we had shared. The basis for my novel came to me seemingly from out of the blue, and for a little while I felt totally exhilarated. Ideas suddenly seemed to pour in thick and fast, and it was as much as I could do to catch them and put them down on paper. It was very exciting.*

The Ace of Wands, in Alex's case, reflected a sudden flash of inspiration, which often precedes an outburst of creative energy.

Within a reading

The Ace of Wands is a card of inspiration and vision. It represents the creative spark that is essential in order to begin any scheme or venture. The Ace of Wands reflects a time of optimism coupled with the necessary imagination and enthusiasm to get an idea off the ground.

Student comments

ALEX (34) *Having had two volumes of short stories published, I had wanted to move on to a full-length novel for some time. One day I was chatting idly*

GERALDINE (62) *The Ace of Wands reminds me of the moment that started my small gardening business. I was planting up my window boxes in the spring as usual and my neighbour liked the look of them so much she asked me to do hers. The seed idea of doing 'container gardens' was sown and I started thinking about whether it could be a little business I could run from home.*

Geraldine's example is a perfect description of the kind of creative idea that can be born under the influence of the energy of the Ace of Wands.

NAME

DATE

PLACE

TIME

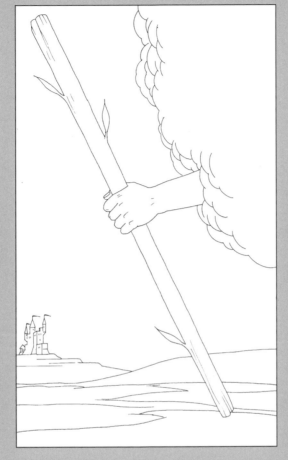

Colouring exercise
Choose colours that you associate with creative energy and positive thought. The Sharman-Caselli deck uses mainly red and yellow for Wands, but you should choose whichever colours mean most to you.

Personal association
Recall a time when you were at the point of starting something new in a creative project or business endeavour. Think of the way the idea came to you – whether it was a bolt from the blue or grew gradually.

What this image means in my life

Readings in which it was significant

See Reading Record Sheet of

ACE *of* SWORDS

The Ace of Swords depicts an upright sword with a wreath made of the olive branch of peace and the palm of victory, which together form a symbol of accomplishment. Swords connect with the intellect and Aces with beginnings, and so together they suggest something new in the realm of thinking. The Swords are often associated with ambivalence due to the fact that the human mind has the unique capacity to formulate ideas for both good and evil.

ACE *of* SWORDS

to have the operation. I didn't like the idea of going into hospital when I wasn't feeling ill, and I hated the fact that I'd have to put myself through that pain. Although I felt terrible immediately after the operation, I no longer have to endure regular bouts of debilitating tonsillitis. I associate this with the Ace of Swords because I made a rational decision to inflict pain on myself with my eye on future benefits.

This is an interesting interpretation of the Ace of Swords, which shows that something positive can emerge out of a painful situation.

Within a reading

The Ace of Swords points to strength in adversity or a situation which initially looks unpromising yet has a positive outcome. This card is usually associated with a sense of the inevitability of great change. Although this change may initially be unwelcome, it is ultimately beneficial.

Student comments

CARA (24) *This card reminds me of making the decision to have my tonsils taken out! I had suffered for years with dreadful tonsillitis, and finally decided*

JAMES (33) *I associate the Ace of Swords with changing jobs. I was doing quite well in the law firm where I worked but not really enjoying it much. Another opportunity arose in a surprising way when I was offered a position in a new field. It was quite a risk to take but somehow I knew it was the right path to follow. I haven't regretted it so far, although it was a very difficult decision to take at the time.*

The Ace of Swords often heralds a time of change, even though that change may involve difficult decisions.

NAME

PLACE

DATE

TIME

Colouring exercise
Colour the image with whichever colours remind you of change. Pay special attention to what the two sides of the sword might mean as well as reflecting on the symbolism of the palm and the olive branch.

Personal association
Try to think of a personal situation that conjures up the meaning of this card for you. Can you think of a time in your life when you had to make a difficult decision that involved changing your life for the better?

What this image means in my life _____

_____

_____

_____

Readings in which it was significant _____

_____

_____

_____

See Reading Record Sheet of _____

ACE *of* PENTACLES

The Ace of Pentacles shows a hand appearing from the left side of creativity, offering a single golden pentacle. The Pentacles are connected with the material world. Here this is symbolized by the garden, partly tame and partly wild, stretching out into the distance. This earthy suit offers lessons in managing practical matters, including financial and physical health. Keeping things in proportion is key to balance in the material world. The hedge around the flowerbeds stands for necessary boundaries to avoid excesses.

ACE *of* PENTACLES

appeared I felt heartened, thinking it might mean money. I could hardly believe it when the following week I received a letter and a cheque from an old aunt I hardly knew. She had decided to give away her money to all her relatives before she died! I was surprised and amused at the literal translation of the Ace of Pentacles.

SUSAN (51) *I connect the Ace of Pentacles with a time recently when my husband and I needed to find a lump sum to pay for our daughter's wedding. After some careful research, we organized our mortgage to release some capital while lowering our monthly outgoings at the same time. It felt like a gift, although technically we were paying for it. The effect it had on our lives was to give us a sense of financial freedom.*

Within a reading

The Ace in the earthy suit of Pentacles represents potential for financial propositions or business ventures. It can signify lump sums suddenly being made available, either through shrewd investment or generous gifts.

Student comments

ALEX (34) *The Ace of Pentacles came up in a reading several years ago when I was planning to travel. Although I had worked hard and saved, I was still short of funds. When the Ace of Pentacles*

These examples demonstrate some of the different ways this card can be experienced. In Alex's case it brought an actual gift, while in Susan's it brought a financial boost which felt like a gift. The Ace of Pentacles symbolizes the material or practical gain that is sometimes needed in life, whether for pleasure or to start a new business venture.

NAME

DATE

PLACE

TIME

Colouring exercise
As you colour this image, think about the earth and all aspects of the earthy element. Consider the different types of flowers and what they represent, such as roses for passion and lilies for purity.

Personal association
Reflect on your own experiences in matters of finance. Think about what money means to you and how you use it, then apply that to the Ace of Pentacles as a symbol of new beginnings.

What this image means in my life

Readings in which it was significant

See Reading Record Sheet of

TWO *of* CUPS

The image shows a man and a woman exchanging cups. The number Two emphasizes the difference within opposites yet seeks balance between them. The woman's dress is embroidered with white lilies, symbolizing the spirit, while the man's tunic is decorated with red roses, standing for passionate desire.

TWO *of* CUPS

Within a reading

The Two of Cups combines the balance of the number Two with the watery, feeling nature of the suit of Cups to symbolize co-operation, sharing and friendship. This could signify the beginning of a love affair or platonic friendship. There is usually a sense of attraction at the start of a relationship, and often we are attracted to qualities opposite to our own – hence the image of masculine and feminine, which can also be seen as positive and negative, yin and yang.

Student comments

CARA (24) *This card makes me think of my best friend at university. We had rooms next to each other and instantly became great friends, even though we could not have been more different. I am essentially reserved and rather introverted while she is outgoing and extroverted, but together we made a great team. She got us out into the social scene while I calmed everything down when things got too hectic. She influenced me to get out into life, while I encouraged her to be more peaceful and relaxed.*

Cara's example shows the balancing quality associated with the Two of Cups.

JAMES (33) *The Two of Cups reminds me of the beginning of a relationship with a girl who remains an extremely significant figure in my life. We met several years ago at an evening class. There was certainly some physical attraction yet we were both strangely resistant to progressing to a sexual relationship. We became extremely close friends and did not want to change that by becoming lovers in case it spoiled the friendship. She will always be a central figure in my life and, even though we are both now in other committed relationships, our friendship still endures.*

This is a good example of how a platonic relationship is also a reflection of the energy of the Two of Cups.

NAME

PLACE

DATE

TIME

Colouring exercise
As you colour this image, reflect on the balance between the two opposites. Think, also, about the background of the card and the colours you want to symbolize the masculine and feminine.

Personal association
Match the meaning of this card to situations in your own life. Think about the nature of significant relationships and remember how they started. As you become accustomed to relating the divinatory meanings of the cards to your own life, you will become more confident when doing readings.

What this image means in my life ⎯⎯⎯⎯⎯⎯⎯⎯⎯⎯⎯⎯⎯⎯⎯⎯⎯⎯⎯⎯⎯⎯⎯⎯⎯⎯

Readings in which it was significant ⎯⎯⎯⎯⎯⎯⎯⎯⎯⎯⎯⎯⎯⎯⎯⎯⎯⎯⎯⎯⎯⎯⎯⎯

See Reading Record Sheet of ⎯⎯⎯⎯⎯⎯⎯⎯⎯⎯⎯⎯⎯⎯⎯⎯⎯⎯⎯⎯⎯⎯⎯⎯⎯⎯⎯⎯⎯

TWO *of* WANDS

The Two is the number of balanced forces. In the fiery element of Wands it suggests ideas that have been brought to the point of fruition. A man looks out to sea, wearing a cloak and boots, as if ready for a journey. This could be the result of an idea conceived in the Ace of Wands. The balanced forces of action are symbolized by one wand tilting to the right, the side of action, while the other tilts to the left, towards the side of creativity.

TWO *of* WANDS

Within a reading

The Two of Wands describes a situation in which there is more than just a vision – some solid work has been achieved and the project is viable. Although it suggests the early stages of a venture, there is certainly more than just an idea.

Student comments

ALEX (34) *The Two of Wands for me is linked with the groundwork I had to do when writing my novel. After the initial excitement of the idea, which I feel corresponds with the energy of the Ace of Wands, the Two of Wands describes the task that lay ahead in keeping the idea alive while trying to find a structure. I was in that happy place where the project felt fresh and exciting but also real. I was used to false starts and 'pie in the sky' ideas but this felt different.*

Alex aptly describes how the Two can indeed follow the Ace in moving an idea on to the next stage.

GERALDINE (62) *I associate this card with my gardening enterprise mentioned in the Ace. I remember that the initial bright idea, which was energizing and fun, was swiftly followed by the more mundane task of costing the scheme and figuring out how it could work in practice – all the while trying not to lose sight of the original concept. It was certainly harder than simply having the idea, but it still felt very positive nonetheless.*

The Wands represent our dreams and wishes, which are thrilling, but every so often we are obliged to return to earth to make some of the ideas concrete.

NAME

DATE

PLACE

TIME

Colouring exercise
Choose your colours to
reflect fiery energy. Notice
the imagery on the card
that reflects the element,
such as the carved
salamanders – mythical
creatures believed to live
in the heart of a flame.

Personal association
Use the student comments
as a way of getting yourself
thinking about what this
card might mean to you.
Discuss the possible
meaning with friends or
clients who pull this card
in a reading.

What this image means in my life _____

_____

_____

_____

Readings in which it was significant _____

_____

_____

_____

See Reading Record Sheet of _____

TWO *of* SWORDS

The balanced Two in the airy Swords, connected with thinking, depicts a scene of some tension. The perfectly balanced swords cross over the figure's heart, indicating that the feelings are blocked out. Behind her the sea is rough, suggesting turbulent emotions, while birds and butterflies symbolize the element of air. The woman is blindfolded, which suggests there are things she does not want to see.

TWO *of* SWORDS

Within a reading

The Two of Swords indicates a tense situation. There is reluctance about looking at it too closely for fear of having to alter the status quo. The blindfold symbolizes resistance to change. The woman covers her eyes and her heart in the hope that difficulties, if unseen, will go away.

Student comments

SUSAN (51) *The Two of Swords reminds me of a time when my son was very depressed at university and I pretended to myself that nothing was happening. It took me a while to face the truth, which was that it was not a teenage phase but he had* some serious psychological problems. His sister finally pointed out the reality to me and I took off my blindfold and began to act. I still remember the paralysing fear, which gripped me so tightly and made me want to deny the situation absolutely. Once things were out in the open, it was a lot easier for us all.

The Two of Swords reflects something unpleasant so we use the age-old defence mechanism of denial to deal with such situations.

JAMES (33) *The Two of Swords makes me think of a time when I refused to recognize what was happening in my first serious love relationship. I was young and madly in love with a beautiful girl. I believed she loved me too, and certainly did not want to see what was going on with her and my closest friend. Even though I think I 'knew' somewhere inside that they were in love but hiding it from me, I doggedly refused to allow myself to see the reality. When it finally came out I was hurt, but not really surprised.*

James did not want to look at the 'rocks of hard fact' which jut out of the sea behind the blindfolded woman.

NAME

DATE

PLACE

TIME

Colouring exercise
As you colour in this image, think of themes involving unease. Be aware of the clues offered in the image: the new moon suggesting mounting tension, the rough water in the background and the blustery wind.

Personal association
Bring to mind your own experiences of wanting to push something unpleasant away. Try to think of situations in your life when you did not want to know something that was clearly happening.

What this image means in my life _____

_____

_____

_____

Readings in which it was significant _____

_____

_____

_____

See Reading Record Sheet of _____

TWO *of* PENTACLES

The duality of Two in the earthy Pentacles translates into a need to keep finances in some sort of equilibrium. The figure on the card is juggling two pentacles as an image of keeping money moving. In the background two ships, representing his fortune, are negotiating choppy waters. While not serious, there is an air of tension here around financial matters.

TWO *of* PENTACLES

Within a reading

The Two of Pentacles reflects a time when tension exists in the financial or practical side of life. However, it is a situation that is manageable. There is likely to be some financial fluctuation but not disaster.

Student Comments

SUSAN (51) *My husband and I are both freelance workers and we live much of our life in the Two of Pentacles mode, fluctuating between doing a lot of work and making quite good money and fearing that the work sources have dried up. We are quite adept at managing the duality of our financial lives, borrowing in lean times and paying back*

in the good. The Two of Pentacles and the Two of Swords differ in that, with the Pentacles, I am not afraid so I face the reality, while the Two of Swords reflects me in a more anxious mood when I feel paralysed with fear.

Susan is right to distinguish the difference between the Two as experienced when channelled through the airy suit of Swords and the earthy, pragmatic Pentacles.

GERALDINE (62) *I can relate the Two of Pentacles to the financial circumstances I was in when I first set up my gardening business. The idea and the 'how to' were certainly one side of the business but the vexed question of financing it seems very relevant to the Two of Pentacles' energy. I had to borrow money from the bank as well as sell some furniture to make sure I had sufficient capital to buy all my initial equipment. It was a bit fraught at times yet there was also a positive feeling of achievement, which I associate with the Two of Pentacles.*

Geraldine's example of borrowing from one source to pay another is an apt reflection of this card's energy.

NAME

DATE

PLACE

TIME

Colouring exercise
Choose colours that you associate with the positive, practical energy of earth. The Sharman-Caselli deck uses greens and browns to reflect nature and connect this card to the material side of life. You can choose your own.

Personal association
Make a note of your own associations with the Two of Pentacles. Think of times when you have had to juggle and take risks. How do you feel about those times?

What this image means in my life _____

_____

_____

_____

Readings in which it was significant _____

_____

_____

_____

See Reading Record Sheet of _____

THREE *of* CUPS

The image on the Three of Cups is one of joy and festivity. The Three is the number of initial completion so, when combined with the suit representing feelings, it results in an occasion worthy of celebration. The wreaths of flowers around the girls' waists and hair suggest a special occasion or a time for observing ritual ceremony in celebration of a special event.

Within a reading

This card is traditionally linked with celebrations of an emotional nature such as birthdays, engagements, weddings or anniversaries. It conveys a sense of culmination after great effort. Before an event can be celebrated there has to be hard work or input of some kind, and the Three of Cups points to the end result.

Student comments

CARA (24) *This card reminds me of the amazing party I had for my 21st birthday. My parents decided on a big celebration and really went to town. We had such fun choosing the food, drink, music and of course the clothes, and thank goodness it was a success. It marked the threshold from child to adult, an important stage for both my parents and me to recognize. I have always been very close*

THREE *of* CUPS

to my family and we used the party as a symbol of the change that was happening to us all as I formally 'grew up'.

Cara's description of her experience of this card is an apt one. A formal family gathering is a traditional reflection of the Three of Cups, which can also be seen in weddings and christenings.

ALEX (34) *Strangely, my thoughts on this card take me to a different place altogether, to a recent event which has been profoundly meaningful in a truly bittersweet way: my father's funeral. My father was an unusual man blessed with many creative talents but also a big heart. His funeral was a sea of family and dear friends joining together to celebrate his life. The overriding emotion at his funeral was gratitude towards a man who had given generously in so many ways. I was deeply moved at how much love and kindness he had generated in those he left behind. His life was complete and now I want to learn how to live as intensely as he did.*

These different associations with the same card illustrate the many ways each card may be interpreted while keeping the main theme in mind. In the suit of Cups, this theme is emotional.

NAME

PLACE

DATE

TIME

Colouring exercise
Use colours to express the emotions this card evokes in you.

Personal association
Think of emotional situations and celebrations in your life that marked the culmination of great effort. Discuss the card's imagery with friends and clients to discover further associations.

What this image means in my life _____

_____

_____

_____

Readings in which it was significant _____

_____

_____

_____

See Reading Record Sheet of _____

THREE *of* WANDS

The Three of Wands signifies the completion of the first stage of an endeavour. The image shows a man standing at the water's edge looking out to a new horizon. Three wands are fixed firmly in the ground. He uses one as support while looking out towards three ships – representing his ideas – as they make their way to the mysterious pyramids, which symbolize wisdom and knowledge. The Three of initial completion combines with the fiery vision of the suit of Wands. This results in a sense of having reached a place you thought would be the end to discover it is only a beginning.

THREE *of* WANDS

ware program to link keyboard to computer so I could make CDs of my music. I didn't realize how enormously complex the program was. The range of things I needed to learn was huge, and suddenly a whole new range of sound possibilities opened up. The Three of Wands reminds me that my initial thought was simply to get the equipment to do the work, whereas in fact the equipment took me down a new path into an area of musical and technical expertise which has proved fascinating.

It is typical of the Three of Wands to make you realize that what you thought would be the end of a journey is, in actual fact, just a beginning.

Within a reading

The Three of Wands suggests that what was initially going to be the end now turns out to be another starting point. This can be disappointing or exciting, depending how you look at it. The Wands as a fiery and optimistic element tend to see it as a further opportunity.

Student comments

CARA (24) *I love music and am always writing music and songs on my keyboard. I wanted a soft-*

GERALDINE (62) *I keep associating the Wands with my gardening business but it is appropriate because I had to keep refining and changing my ideas as the business progressed. Initially I thought that window boxes and small containers would be a creative yet manageable little business, but once that proved successful I started thinking about bigger gardens. I ended up doing a course in landscape gardening. The window boxes suddenly seemed rather limited and I found myself wanting to learn more and have greater scope.*

NAME

DATE

PLACE

TIME

Colouring exercise
As you colour this image, allow your thoughts to wander to times when you felt this sense of arriving, only to discover you were just beginning.

Personal association
Use this card to help you think of your own story and how your life has taken different turns. Ask others to tell you their experiences that reflect the message of the Three of Wands.

What this image means in my life _____

_____

_____

_____

Readings in which it was significant _____

_____

_____

_____

See Reading Record Sheet of _____

THREE *of* SWORDS

The image on this card suggests pain. A heart pierced with swords in a stained-glass window represents a vision of sorrow – there is an understanding that some sort of pain must be endured. The Three of Swords often means that a situation comes to a head and action must be taken to change things. Although painful, there are times when we must face the truth and act accordingly.

THREE *of* SWORDS

Within a reading

When this card appears in a reading, it may point to an experience of disappointment or sadness. However, there is often a profound understanding that some pain is unavoidable – that it is inevitable and even right.

Student comments

SUSAN (51) *I connect this card with the grief I experienced at my mother's death. We were very close and I was distraught when she developed cancer. She fought bravely, had all the treatments but I gradually realized she would not recover. During her illness I kept hoping and convincing myself that* she would be all right, a feeling I associate with the Two of Swords. That was a tense time. When she died and was finally released from the agony she was suffering, there was a sense of relief alongside the ache of missing her.

The Three of Swords does not signify physical death any more than any of the other cards. However, loss through death could well be associated with this card, as could any other loss, as illustrated in Geraldine's example below. The tarot should never be taken literally but rather used as an aid to understanding the wide spectrum of human emotions and experience.

GERALDINE (62) *I connect this card with my daughter leaving home. As a single mother, my relationship with my only daughter was very close, so when she left home I felt very lonely. I knew it was right and proper for her to be independent, and I was truly glad for her on that level. Nevertheless, my own selfish desire for her company made the separation hard. I really understand the paradox in the Three of Swords of a painful situation which is, yet, right and which needs to be like that.*

NAME

DATE

PLACE

TIME

Colouring exercise
Choose colours you
associate with difficult
times. As you colour in
the image, notice that the
clouds are whiter behind
the pierced heart although
the edges are grey.

Personal association
Think of a time in your life
when something changed
or was lost. How did you
deal with it? While you
should recognize the
inevitability of sorrow in
life, also consider the ways
wounds can be healed and
damage repaired.

What this image means in my life _____

_____

_____

_____

Readings in which it was significant _____

_____

_____

_____

See Reading Record Sheet of _____

THREE *of* PENTACLES

This card shows a workman leaving a job where the structure is complete but the work is not finished. The Three of Pentacles suggests that things have been achieved but there is still work to be done. Once again, the initial completion suggested by the Three shows that the basic structure is sound but the finishing touches remain outstanding.

THREE *of* PENTACLES

Within a reading

This card denotes some sort of material accomplishment that has been gained through hard work and perseverance. Even though it is not yet finished, it is worthy of recognition and a sense of achievement.

Student comments

JAMES (33) *This card makes me think of buying my first flat. Raising the mortgage money was a nerve-wracking business. When the transaction was over it felt as if I had climbed a mountain. I clearly remember sitting in an empty flat feeling a great sense of satisfaction, even though I was acutely aware of all the work I needed to do on the place.*

That experience brings home to me the notion of initial completion. James's example is typical: a structure exists and now the rest needs to be done. In the case of a flat the obvious fixtures, fittings and furnishings need to be gathered before the home is complete, but the important initial completion represented by the Three of Pentacles is the acquisition of the structure.

SUSAN (51) *This card reminds me of the bed-and-breakfast cottage my husband and I started when we were first married. It took us a while to find the right property and even longer to set the whole thing up. We had all the rooms organized, everything was ready and all we had to do then was wait for the finishing touches, which in our case were the guests! For us the initial completion was getting the physical structure of the place ready, and for the next stage to happen we needed bookings.*

These examples show how different people can have different experiences of the same basic theme of initial completion.

NAME

DATE

PLACE

TIME

Colouring exercise
Choose colours that make
you feel grounded and in
touch with the earthy
nature of this suit. Use
whichever colours most
clearly represent the
natural world for you.

Personal association
Use your own experiences
of the initial completion
of a project to associate
something personal with
the Three of Pentacles.
Discuss this with clients
or friends to get some of
their ideas too and see how
many different associations
can be made.

What this image means in my life

Readings in which it was significant

See Reading Record Sheet of

FOUR *of* CUPS

The Four of Cups reflects the notion of discontent. A disconsolate youth sits with arms and legs crossed as if trying to ward off uncomfortable feelings. He stares sulkily at three full cups in front of him as if they are not giving him what he wants while ignoring the cup offered from the hand on the right of the image – the side of action. It is an image of discontent and disappointment rather than tragedy or acute misery. Four is the number of reality and solidity, which does not combine comfortably with the fluid, watery Cups.

FOUR *of* CUPS

Within a reading

The Four of Cups describes a sense of dissatisfaction on an emotional level with one's lot in life. Even with little in reality to warrant such discontent, there is nevertheless a sense of futility or depression coming from within. This card suggests a feeling of boredom and even a refusal to make an effort to improve the situation.

Student comments

SUSAN (51) *I associate this card with post-natal depression. I had longed to be a mother, but after the birth I felt trapped, bored and lonely at home with my son, yet too depressed to take up any offers of help. I felt let down, even cheated, that my becoming a mother had not automatically made everything wonderful. I believed motherhood would magically change any wrongs in my marriage, my life and myself. It took some time to move out of that resentful, dissatisfied place, which is partly why I remember it so clearly.*

It is not uncommon for the triumphant feeling associated with the initial completion of the Threes to give way to a sense of dissatisfaction when the reality of the Fours becomes apparent.

GERALDINE (62) *I associate this card with the time after my honeymoon. I remember having had a wonderful wedding with lots of presents and feeling very excited. Then, on honeymoon, thinking, 'Oh God, what have I done? Who is this man? Do I really want to live with him for the rest of my life?' The worst thing was that everyone kept being terribly pleased for me and saying what a lovely new home we had and how happy I must be, while inside I was feeling rather flat and depressed.*

Geraldine's experience is a good example of how everything can look good from the outside but does not necessarily match up with how one feels on the inside.

NAME

DATE

PLACE

TIME

Colouring exercise
Choose colours that you associate with feelings. As you colour the image, try to identify with the central figure, paying attention to the body language and facial expression.

Personal association
Think of times when you have had no real reason to complain yet still felt down or depressed. How do you resolve such situations? Do you allow yourself to slide further into depression or do you find ways to lift yourself out? Through discussion, see how others respond to the mood captured in this image.

What this image means in my life _____

_____

_____

_____

Readings in which it was significant _____

_____

_____

_____

See Reading Record Sheet of _____

FOUR *of* WANDS

When combined with number Four, the fiery suit of Wands is happier than the emotional Cups. The solidity of the Four translates the creativity of the Wands into reality. The image shows a homecoming hero – the same figure as in the Two and Three of Wands – complete with garlands and welcoming crowd.

Within a reading

The Four of Wands suggests a time of relaxation and deserved reward after a period of strain. Although it is not a time that can last indefinitely, there is nonetheless a sense of appreciation and fulfilment for a break that follows hard work and effort. Something worthy of celebration has been achieved so a reward is deserved.

Student comments

CARA (24) *This reminds me of the holiday I took after my exams before going on to university. I had worked really hard to get good grades, so the sense of relief and alleviation of pressure was wonderful. At first it was odd not to have to get up and*

FOUR *of* WANDS

start studying, but once that penny dropped I threw myself into enjoying the holiday, fully aware that it would have to end in the autumn when I started at university. I strongly felt 'Enjoy this while you can, because it is only for now', which is a feeling I associate with the Four of Wands.

SUSAN (51) *I associate this card with the ending of the summer term while my children were at school. Those terms were always full of exams, prize-giving and end-of-term plays, so by the time they came to an end we were all exhausted. The feeling of a long holiday ahead was absolutely wonderful. Perhaps the holidays were so special because we knew they would end, but we certainly enjoyed them to the full. I miss that routine of hard work followed by rest now they are no longer at school.*

Both examples describe the sense of relief and relaxation after hard work, together with the knowledge that it is not a permanent state. This is typical of the energy of the Four of Wands.

NAME

DATE

PLACE

TIME

Colouring exercise
Choose colours that call
to mind a joyful occasion
or suggest a mood of
celebration. As you colour,
turn your imagination
loose and familiarize
yourself with the card's
imagery.

Personal association
Think about your own
experiences of work, rest
and play. Bring to mind
as many examples from
your life as you can, then
add others' experiences
to your list.

What this image means in my life _____

_____

_____

_____

Readings in which it was significant _____

_____

_____

_____

See Reading Record Sheet of _____

FOUR *of* SWORDS

The overall impression of this image is one of peace and quiet. In the number Four, the energy of the Swords, which so often represent tension or anxiety, is tranquil and calm. The figure symbolizes a deep and healing sleep, rather than death. After any upset, heartbreak or illness, we all need time for recovery and recuperation. This image represents 'time out' from ordinary life to mend or heal.

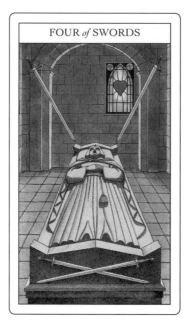

FOUR *of* SWORDS

Within a reading

This card suggests the need for a time of solitude and contemplation. The Four of Swords is the card of convalescence as it symbolizes the time needed to recover after stress and upset, which may be caused by relationship problems or perhaps work difficulties. It is essential to allow time to convalesce, especially in our modern society where there is so much pressure on us just to 'get on with it'.

Student comments

GERALDINE (62) *I associate this card with the time after my divorce. The separation and move out of the marital home was very traumatic but I tried to carry on, ignoring both my body and my emotions. Eventually I became really ill and collapsed, which meant I finally had to take the rest I desperately needed. I had to allow myself the time, space and solitude to grieve and heal, both my heart and my body.*

ALEX (34) *I have fond associations with this card because it reminds me of a time of convalescence after I injured my knee seriously and had to have a number of operations. I was forced to be still for some months which, in turn, forced me to think more and also to read a lot. In fact, that time of reading and reflection laid the groundwork for my wish to write. I had never given myself too much time for reading until then – I was always far too busy rushing around. Although it's a cliché, a 'new world' really did open up for me.*

The notion of convalescence seems rather old-fashioned these days, as people are in a constant rush to 'get on, get well or get over it'. Nevertheless, as these examples illustrate, it is essential to our physical and psychological well-being, and – as in Alex's case – can also have a lasting benefit.

NAME

DATE

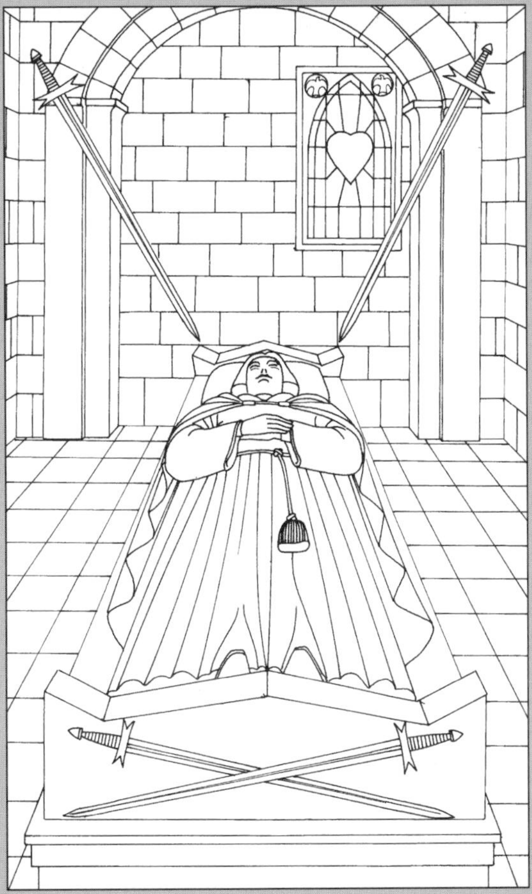

PLACE

TIME

Colouring exercise
This image is peaceful yet suggests a time to gather strength and recharge batteries. Choose calming, quiet colours.

Personal association
Take time to consider your own views on the need for convalescence and recuperation. How do you deal with yourself when you are ill, tired or emotionally depleted? What does this image mean to you?

What this image means in my life _____

Readings in which it was significant _____

See Reading Record Sheet of _____

FOUR *of* PENTACLES

The number Four of solidity and the earthy element of Pentacles combine to produce an image of trapped energy. A man sits on the lid of a fine trunk clasping a pentacle close to his heart in a defensive manner. He appears fearful of losing his precious possessions. This card points out the dangers of stagnation of emotional or financial energy, which may have the overall effect of no loss, but no gain either.

FOUR *of* PENTACLES

Within a reading

The Four of Pentacles suggests a fear of loss, which may in fact have the effect of inhibiting gain. On one level it may refer to material possessions, while on another level it suggests that the way money is handled may link with emotional dealings. This card, therefore, can represent a tendency to be 'tight' with money or emotions. Traditionally it is known as the card of the miser.

Student comments

ALEX (34) *This card makes me aware of my fear of sharing ideas with other writers. I am afraid they will either steal my best ideas or make me feel bad about my work. I know I would benefit from discussion groups or workshops, and I know*

I am in danger of cutting off my proverbial nose to spite my face, but I'm too afraid of 'letting go'. I associate the Four of Pentacles with miserliness, and although I am rather uncomfortable about admitting that quality in myself, I am nevertheless afraid that it is there around my work. I don't tend to have a problem regarding meanness with money, but I do think I am guilty of being mean with my ideas.

SUSAN (51) *This card reminds me of how I feel when we are insecure with money, which goes back to my childhood when we were quite poor. Today my husband and I make enough money but because we are freelance there are inevitably hard times, and these make me anxious. At such times I won't spend any money at all, even on advertising, which is really silly as that is the way to bring in new work. The fear of financial loss makes me very tense, so I hang on to everything tightly, even though I know it actually prevents things from moving and flowing.*

Alex identifies his miserliness with ideas and creativity, while Susan's example is more concretely about material matters. Both are equally valid.

NAME

DATE

PLACE

TIME

Colouring exercise
As you colour this image, pay attention to the symbolism of the card. Try to feel the tight grip as the man holds his pentacle and see if it reflects any of your own feelings.

Personal association
Call to mind any associations with this card you can find in your life experience. Think of how you act when threatened in any way, whether it be financially or emotionally.

What this image means in my life _____

_____

_____

_____

Readings in which it was significant _____

_____

_____

_____

See Reading Record Sheet of _____

FIVE *of* CUPS

The image of the Five of Cups is clearly one of sadness. A solitary figure wearing black robes of mourning bows over three overturned cups, symbolizing what is lost. No attention is paid to the remaining full cups, which stand for what remains intact. A bridge over the river of sorrow in the distance indicates the way forward.

FIVE *of* CUPS

Within a reading

The Five of Cups describes the feeling of sadness, loss or disappointment when something one cares for is lost or spoilt. It is difficult to see remaining positives but they do exist, symbolized here by the full cups behind the grieving figure.

Student comments

CARA (24) *This card reminds me of the ending of my first important love affair. He fell in love with someone else and I was totally devastated. However, once the initial hurt and pain had subsided and I had found a new boyfriend, we discovered we had enough left between us to form a really close friendship. This was because the relationship was deep and involved genuine mutual liking as well as physical attraction. We are still good friends now. I think of that as the full cups and the break-up as the spilled cups.*

GERALDINE (62) *This card makes me think of the break-up of my marriage. It was a painful time as my husband left me for a new relationship and I felt deeply humiliated and hurt. For a while I wanted to punish my husband and cut him out of my life completely, but in time I had to acknowledge that we did have the equivalent of full cups in our daughter, whom we both love dearly. It was through my desire not to let her suffer as a result of our failed marriage that we finally established a way of communicating and relating to one another that was reasonably amicable despite the deep sense of hurt, especially on my part.*

It is clear from both these examples that some sort of reconciliation or level of communication can be achieved even when something has gone wrong in a relationship. When this happens, it makes the pain more bearable.

NAME

DATE

PLACE

TIME

Colouring exercise
When colouring this image, pay close attention to all the symbolism, such as the bridge showing the way across and over difficult times and the castle standing for something to aim for in the future.

Personal association
Draw on your own experience of loss and gain to get a better understanding of this card's meaning. See how relevant this card is to you, then test it on others to get a fuller picture.

What this image means in my life _____

_____

_____

_____

Readings in which it was significant _____

_____

_____

_____

See Reading Record Sheet of _____

FIVE *of* WANDS

The Five of Wands is an image of struggle and conflict. The Five is a number of uncertainty and inconstancy. In combination with the fiery element of the Wands it suggests difficulty in the realm of creativity and imagination.

Within a reading

The Five of Wands suggests a time when creative progress is either slow or obstructed, perhaps by external forces or through inner blocks and inhibitions. It might reflect a time when financial or practical hardships can hinder headway in the realm of creativity or artistic pursuit, or when inner resources are at a low point and nothing seems to quite work out.

Student comments

ALEX (34) *This card illustrates the way I felt during the middle part of writing my book. The first bit was easy when ideas flooded in and I felt excited and positive. Then came a tremendous feeling of inertia when I could hardly muster the enthusiasm to write a single word. I felt as though I was wading through treacle. It was literally all*

FIVE *of* WANDS

I could do just to keep going with the project. I felt stuck and stale and was quite convinced that any talent or inspiration had deserted me forever. It was a very frustrating period.

CARA (24) *The Five of Wands reminds me of my last year at university when I was struggling to write my final dissertation. I had plenty of ideas, loads of research and was keen to get on with it, but I was beset by endless problems on a practical level. My living quarters were under threat, as the landlord suddenly decided he wanted to sell our rented house and we became involved in time-consuming legal problems. I was short of money and had to work in a bar, which took my focus away from written work. I wanted to write the dissertation but felt constantly undermined by aggravating practical details and lost the creative impetus I needed.*

The Five of Wands describes blocked creativity, either when inspiration deserts us as in Alex's case, or as in Cara's when the real world impinges and prevents the flow of imagination.

NAME

DATE

PLACE

TIME

Colouring exercise
Try to get in touch with
the sense of struggle
depicted in this image as
you select colours for it.
Notice that one of the men
is barefoot, emphasizing
his vulnerability. They are
fighting hand-to-hand
with crossed wands,
symbolizing creative
blocks.

Personal association
Think about any situation
in which you felt frustrated
in your creative desires.
Try to recall such feelings
and write them down.

What this image means in my life _____

_____

_____

_____

Readings in which it was significant _____

_____

_____

_____

See Reading Record Sheet of _____

FIVE *of* SWORDS

The Five of Swords conjures up an ambivalent image. Five is the number of tension. In the suit of Swords it reveals problems that arise both when one is triumphant and when one is defeated. The figure in the foreground is clearly victorious, while in the distance two men bow their heads in failure. They have surrendered their weapons and walk away, recognizing the fact that their opponent was too powerful. The defeat is not life-threatening and, although humiliated, they will survive.

FIVE *of* SWORDS

Within a reading

This card suggests it would be wise to think carefully about a situation before deciding to tackle it. If you really cannot win, it may be better to be aware of this from the outset and not enter the fray. Try to recognize when a fight cannot be won and not waste precious resources.

Student comments

JAMES (33) *This card reminds me of school. My parents wanted me to study medicine but my heart wasn't in it. Although I am not stupid, sciences were not my strong subjects – I am much better suited to the arts. Consequently I did badly in my exams and was not accepted for medical school. Now I regret the time I wasted struggling with subjects I could never excel at instead of enjoying being able to concentrate on something that I could actually do well.*

SUSAN (51) *This card reminds me of when we first married and set up a bed-and-breakfast business against the advice of friends and professionals. We were warned about the difficulties but ignored them all. We did not prosper and finally had to sell. Although, fortunately, we didn't lose too badly, we certainly learned a lesson in humility. I realize there are genuine limitations in life and the real trick is to try to figure out what I can and can't do. I see the Five of Swords as facing up to and working with my own limits. This is not about being lazy or unnecessarily humble – just realistic.*

This card points to the wisdom of recognizing one's own boundaries and limitations, as illustrated by James and Susan.

NAME

PLACE

DATE

TIME

Colouring exercise
Choose your own colours for this card as you reflect on what the image means to you. Place yourself in the position of both the victor and the defeated and remember how it feels in both places.

Personal association
Think of situations in your own life when you tackled something too big for you. Reflect on issues concerning the acceptance of limitations and the confines of your own personal destiny.

What this image means in my life _____

_____

_____

_____

Readings in which it was significant _____

_____

_____

_____

See Reading Record Sheet of _____

FIVE *of* PENTACLES

The suit of Pentacles suggests earthy reliability, yet the Five is an inconstant number, so the combination of the two results in material or financial instability. Two beggars huddle in the snow outside a lighted church window. The window represents sanctuary, but neither figure appears to notice the potential shelter. The image suggests more than poverty. It points to a loss of personal esteem or spiritual values, which may ultimately be worse.

FIVE *of* PENTACLES

Within a reading

The Five of Pentacles may point to a time of financial hardship or loss of money, sometimes accompanied by a loss of faith or loss of self-worth. While financial problems are uncomfortable, they are bearable if we do not lose faith or self-respect.

Student comments

SUSAN (51) *This card reminds me of when my husband was made redundant suddenly with very little redundancy pay. Not only did he feel angry, he also felt humiliated and a failure. The financial*

crisis was real but so was the loss of self-esteem. It is hard to say now, looking back, which was worse. After the initial shock, however, when we had to face loss of status among friends and colleagues, my husband retrained and established himself in a new field through sheer determination.

GERALDINE (62) *For me, the Five of Pentacles reflects my feelings after my daughter was born. Until then I had been financially independent but I stopped work and relied on my husband's income. I started to feel insecure about my financial position, as my husband tended to make a big deal about giving me money. I was suddenly without status or financial power. Without a career and my own financial security I felt as if I wasn't worth anything. It was a time in my life when I suppose I should have been happy and fulfilled – and on one level I was – but I was also beset with insecurity and a loss of self-esteem.*

Susan's example shows one way in which the Five of Pentacles could work, while Geraldine's indicates another equally valid description of this card's energy.

NAME

PLACE

DATE

TIME

Colouring exercise
As you choose colours for this image, think about the beggars in the snow and about how difficult it is to stay hopeful in times of financial crisis. Understanding these feelings in yourself will help you empathize with others when you do readings.

Personal association
Think about times in your life when you lost money or hope. How did that affect the way you felt about yourself?

What this image means in my life _____

_____

_____

_____

Readings in which it was significant _____

_____

_____

_____

See Reading Record Sheet of _____

SIX *of* CUPS

Six is a number that suggests equilibrium. Combined with the feeling-oriented suit of Cups, it symbolizes a time in which memories and events from the past are significant. The cottage garden nostalgically evokes childhood dreams and wishes while the dwarf, a symbol of the past, works in harmony with a child, a symbol of the future, suggesting that past and future are linked by efforts in the present.

SIX *of* CUPS

Within a reading

The Six of Cups signifies that long-held dreams or wishes from the past come to fruition in the present. Because the Cups are connected with feelings, this card suggests that relationships with roots in the past may revive in the present, bringing hope for the future.

Student comments

CARA (24) *This card reminds me of meeting an old friend at university, a girl I had been 'best friends' with at primary school. Her family moved away and we lost touch. In fact, I hardly remembered her until we bumped into each other at university, where we discovered that we happened to be doing the same degree. Our friendship, interrupted for fourteen years, started up again as if we had always known each other, and still continues even though we have now both graduated and moved on with our careers.*

GERALDINE (62) *For me the Six of Cups brings to mind an extraordinary chance encounter with an old friend I had known when we both lived abroad as teenagers. I had moved back to England and we lost contact completely. Many years later in a busy shopping street in central London, I happened to be looking in a shop window and realized she was standing right next to me! It was the most amazing coincidence and actually seemed quite fated, as she was in a difficult situation and urgently needed help. I was only too delighted to see my old friend again and be able to offer her support. We are still friends now.*

These are both good examples of something with roots in the past bearing positive fruit in the present in surprising ways. Sometimes the past can catch up with us in less fortunate ways, so it is worth considering both options to get a good sense of this card.

NAME

DATE

PLACE

TIME

Colouring exercise
Use the colours you feel
best conjure up the past
for you. As you colour in
this image, contemplate the
notion that what happens
in our present always has
roots in the past.

Personal association
To try recall events in
your life when things
that seemed to be part of
the past were suddenly
rekindled or reappeared in
your present. Think about
the positive and negative
side of such possibilities.

What this image means in my life _____

_____

_____

_____

Readings in which it was significant _____

_____

_____

_____

See Reading Record Sheet of _____

SIX *of* WANDS

Six is a number of harmony, so in the fiery Wands it represents a positive sense of achievement. The image is one of victory – a smiling man wearing a crown of laurels, symbolizing attainment, raises up a wreath of success in triumph. The overall impression is one of satisfaction, a result of the combination of the Wands' creative energy harmoniously coupled with the balanced Six.

SIX *of* WANDS

Within a reading

This card signifies a moment of public achievement. It suggests a promotion, or a creative project that has been accepted for display or publication. The key point is that the achievement stimulates public acknowledgement or acclaim.

Student comments

JAMES (33) *This card makes me think about the pride I felt when I finally graduated from university with a decent law degree. I had experienced so many setbacks through my school days that reaching the end of my studies with a piece of paper*

worth having was a great result for me. I felt good about it because it was public recognition of my efforts, and I felt it meant I could hold my head up in the job market.

ALEX (34) *The Six of Wands reminds me of seeing my first article in print in a magazine. I remember feeling so strange that something I had written had made its way into a public arena. I felt a mixture of pride and fear, knowing that publication can evoke both positive and negative feedback. Seeing the article in a magazine made me realize the enormity of exposing my views in public, which was both alarming and exciting at the same time.*

The important thing to remember about the Six of Wands is that it signifies an honour conferred by the public at large. This makes it impersonal and objective and therefore a very different experience to a sense of inner personal achievement, as both these examples demonstrate. This is not to say that one is better than the other, only that they are different experiences.

NAME

PLACE

DATE

TIME

Colouring exercise
Use the kind of colours you feel would best represent a situation of triumph and achievement. Try to identify with the sense of accomplishment felt by the central figure, calling to mind times in your own life when you have felt like that.

Personal association
Remember those times in your life when you have achieved something recognized as worthy by the public, especially if it falls into the creative category.

What this image means in my life ⎯⎯⎯⎯⎯⎯⎯⎯⎯⎯⎯⎯⎯⎯⎯⎯⎯⎯⎯⎯

Readings in which it was significant ⎯⎯⎯⎯⎯⎯⎯⎯⎯⎯⎯⎯⎯⎯⎯⎯⎯⎯

See Reading Record Sheet of ⎯⎯⎯⎯⎯⎯⎯⎯⎯⎯⎯⎯⎯⎯⎯⎯⎯⎯⎯⎯⎯

SIX *of* SWORDS

The Six of Swords forms an interesting combination – the harmony of the number Six softens the tension so often found in the suit of Swords. The image indicates a move from difficult times towards more peaceful ones, as the water on one side of the boat is rough while the sea ahead is calm. Overhead the skies are clear, suggesting that the current problems are temporary. The Six is one of the few numbers that reflect harmony in all the suits.

SIX *of* SWORDS

Within a reading

This card suggests a shift from strained or agitated times to something more relaxed and easy-going. This might manifest in a physical move involving a change of residence or job. Alternatively it may describe a move on an inner level when attitudes alter from anxious and apprehensive to calm and confident.

Student comments

ALEX (34) *The Six of Swords makes me think about the change in attitude I have been slowly undergoing since I started therapy to address my panic attacks and anxiety. It hasn't exactly been easy, but I do feel that I am at last getting to the point where the calm waters are in sight. Whereas I used to feel as if I would never get there, I now believe I can – and will – reach a better place inside.*

JAMES (33) *This card makes me think of the physical move I made when I left rented accommodation and bought my own flat. When I lived in a rented flat the area was quite rough and my neighbours were frankly terrifying. The flat was nice inside, but getting to and from home could be a very tense experience. When I was finally able to buy my own flat I made sure that it was in a safe neighbourhood. I didn't have to worry about things like coming home late at night, which made a great deal of difference to my peace of mind.*

The above examples show how the Six of Swords can be experienced on both inner and outer levels. Alex speaks about the difficulty of living with inner tension, while James talks about the outer level. Both are valid and typical of the feelings associated with this card.

NAME

PLACE

DATE

TIME

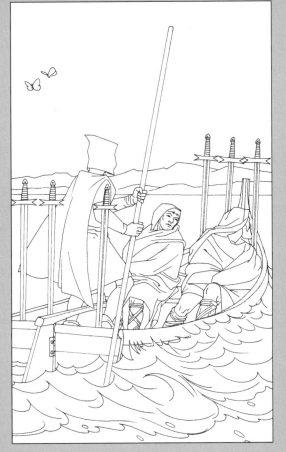

Colouring exercise
Use colours to reflect the contrast between tension and fear and a sense of assurance.

Personal association
Match the meaning of this card to areas of your own experience. Think about times when you have moved out of difficulty and deliberately sought better experiences.

What this image means in my life _____

_____

_____

_____

Readings in which it was significant _____

_____

_____

_____

See Reading Record Sheet of _____

SIX *of* PENTACLES

The earthy suit of Pentacles combines with the harmonious number Six to show an image of money being apportioned evenly to the deserving. A man of means measures out gold equally to the obviously poorer couple before him. He uses scales to measure out the money, suggesting that the riches are being supplied according to need rather than randomly distributed, and he uses his right hand – the active side – to distribute it. The symmetry of the position of the pentacles in the arch suggests equality, while the castle on the hill in the distance symbolizes material security.

SIX *of* PENTACLES

Within a reading

The Six of Pentacles suggests that financial or material help comes in time of genuine need, and must be offered if others need it. The sense of equilibrium symbolized by the Six works both ways – to maintain balanced energy, resources need to be shared with those who need them most. This card does not promise luxury or extravagance but suggests that true needs may be met.

Student comments

JAMES (33) *This card makes me think of when I bought my flat. I had calculated my costs to the last penny and was really upset when the boiler broke down shortly after I moved in. The cost of replacement was a real worry. Then, unexpectedly, I discovered I was entitled to a tax rebate, which amounted almost exactly to the cost of a new boiler. I felt as if I had been given a heavenly break, and although there was nothing to spare I somehow got just what I needed.*

SUSAN (51) *This card reminds me of when I wanted to do another year's full-time course. I had enough money to pay rent and expenses for the year but not enough for the fees. I heard, quite by chance, about an obscure trust in my local London borough which provided a bursary from an ancient benevolent fund set up for young people to participate in higher education. I applied, the trust accepted me and paid the course fees.*

These two examples are typical of this card, which suggests that opportunities arise to enable a specific course of action, rather than to make dreams of huge wealth come true.

NAME

DATE

PLACE

TIME

Colouring exercise
Choose colours that
call to mind a spirit of
kindness and generosity.
Think about the even
distribution of wealth as
you contemplate the man
giving of his plenty to
those in greater need.

Personal association
Think about times in
your life when you have
given to others, or had
things given to you, and
recollect the feelings
that benevolence and
generosity evoke.

What this image means in my life

Readings in which it was significant

See Reading Record Sheet of

SEVEN *of* CUPS

The number Seven represents choices and changes. As it is a profound number, however, changes generally come from within rather than from the external world. Seven combined with the watery element of the Cups results in important choices involving the feelings. The card depicts a man dreaming of different images all encased in clouds, suggesting they are in fantasy and have no base in reality yet. The positive energy of this card is imagination, but some of the fantasy must be made concrete if it is to last beyond the dream.

SEVEN *of* CUPS

Within a reading

The Seven of Cups suggests there are many options available and decisions to be made. Although the suit of Cups is associated with feelings, it is concerned with more than relationships. It relates to matters of deep personal significance, ranging from success, wealth, strength, security and sexual relationships through to spiritual matters and self-discovery.

Student comments

GERALDINE (62) *This card reminds me of how I came to be interested in tarot. I was searching for deeper meaning in my life and considered studying a number of disciplines including graphology, astrology and numerology. I finally decided on tarot after doing a weekend course. Since then I have been studying tarot seriously and, to my delight, it has led to my being able to study some of the other things I was interested in. However, in the beginning I did have to limit myself, which is why I associate that period of choosing with the Seven of Cups.*

CARA (24) *I associate the Seven of Cups with choosing a whole new group of friends when I went to university. I was far away from home and knew no one, so choosing a new social circle represented an important stage in my life. I was aware that my friendship group would probably define the next three years of my life, so I wanted to make like-minded friends who shared my values.*

It is clear from these comments that their choices reflected what was most important to them at the time: Geraldine's choices involved her search for personal meaning and development in life; Cara's involved relationships, which also reflects development, but of a different kind. The Seven of Cups can reflect both.

NAME

PLACE

DATE

TIME

Colouring exercise
As you colour the image, think about all the objects appearing from the cups and try to add images from your own imagination.

Personal association
Think about the feelings that are evoked when you make decisions. Reflect on important choices you have had to make.

What this image means in my life _____

_____

_____

_____

Readings in which it was significant _____

_____

_____

_____

See Reading Record Sheet of _____

SEVEN *of* WANDS

The image on this card reflects the notion of conflict. A man stands alone, defending himself fiercely as if he is in danger of being overpowered and outnumbered. He is battling with stiff competition from the outside world and perhaps with the limitation of his own imagination and creative prowess. While the image is one of battle, it does not portray bloodshed; rather a sense of having to rise to a challenge.

Within a reading

This card describes a creative struggle and stiff competition. The kind of situation reflected here may be in areas of working or creative life, possibly involving some form of advancement or promotion.

Student Comments

CARA (24) *For me the Seven of Wands encapsulates leaving university with a first-class degree and thinking that the world would be eagerly waiting for me to arrive. I was shocked when I went for interviews with other applicants who also had good degrees and sometimes more experience or suitability for the job than I did. I suddenly realized I had to raise my game enormously and compete in a very different arena. It proved a sobering experience, yet once I became accustomed to the new playing field I realized I had better take up the challenge with enthusiasm.*

Cara's experience is typical of the Seven of Wands. The notion that a certain position, whether in work or study, will mean you have 'arrived' and do not need to struggle any more, is a false one.

ALEX (34) *This card makes me think of trying to get my first novel published. I was pleased with it, and some professionals I knew had said it was good too. When I actually sent it out to publishers, however, I found myself in a different world altogether. Many publishers rejected my precious book out of hand, and those who showed a spark of interest wanted it changed and rewritten. I know now that the battering my ego took in the process resulted in a better novel, which, after many agonizing rewrites, was finally published. The Seven of Wands is an apt symbol of how it felt when I was going through the process. I felt as though I was standing alone in the face of competition and suffering humiliating rejection.*

The higher you climb, the tougher the competition you will face. However, this also becomes the spur that drives us on to achieve more worthwhile goals, even though there can certainly be difficult and disheartening moments en route.

NAME

PLACE

DATE

TIME

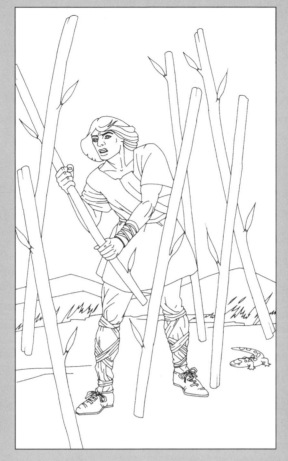

Colouring exercise
Choose your own colours and think about how they reflect what the image means to you. Try to identify with the figure; feel the tension in his clenched fists as he staves off the attacking wands.

Personal association
Match the meaning of the card to events in your life, then ask others for their reactions. The more feedback you can gather on what this card means to you and others, the more you can bring its meaning alive.

What this image means in my life _____

Readings in which it was significant _____

See Reading Record Sheet of _____

SEVEN *of* SWORDS

The sense of knowledge coupled with conscious choices is inherent in the number Seven. Combined with the airy element of the Swords, it produces a certain kind of mental ambivalence. The scene on this card is of a man leaving a tent with an armful of swords. His expression is both gleeful and surreptitious, giving an impression of escape.

SEVEN *of* SWORDS

Within a reading

The Seven of Swords suggests a time for thinking through tactics carefully and employing the intellectual skills associated with the airy suit of Swords. Aggressive and direct approaches may be less effective than diplomatic efforts in whatever situation this card refers to. There is a need for discretion and prudence in achieving aims.

Student comments

JAMES (33) *This card makes me think of a time when I wanted to change jobs but I could hardly announce my intention outright to my employer. I had to be discreet and careful about taking time out from work to attend other interviews as I didn't want to jeopardize my then current position until I was sure that I actually had another job to go to.*

James's situation is typical of the Seven of Swords. It was not in his interests to be completely honest with his employers, so he found himself in the position of being 'economical with the truth' rather than telling an outright lie.

CARA (24) *When I worked in a dress shop in the holidays, people would sometimes ask whether I thought a particular outfit suited them or not. I was careful about what I said and how I said it so that I didn't actually lie, but neither was I completely honest with the customers. It was difficult because I had dilemmas about whether it was any of my business to advise customers on what to choose. There was also the money issue: did I dare advise a customer not to buy something, thus losing my commission? The Seven of Swords makes me think of those kinds of issue.*

Cara's example is also apt because she was struggling with a moral dilemma about telling the truth and her own need or greed for money. The Seven of Swords is an ambivalent card, reflecting 'grey' rather than 'black and white' issues.

NAME

DATE

PLACE

TIME

Colouring exercise
As you colour in the image, try to identify with the figure as he sneaks away from the camp. Feel the conflicting feelings and thoughts that are associated with this card.

Personal association
Can you identify with the student comments on this card? Try to remember times in your life when you have faced similar situations.

What this image means in my life

Readings in which it was significant

See Reading Record Sheet of

SEVEN *of* PENTACLES

The sense of choice evoked in the number Seven is connected here with the earthy suit of Pentacles, suggesting a pause in the development of an enterprise or business. A man stands between a field of ripe maize and a newly planted field. He is looking at the mature field as if he is wondering whether to continue attending to that field or turn his attention to the one which represents fruitfulness in potential rather than in reality.

Within a reading

This card suggests that this is a moment when much has been achieved and it is possible to continue building on it. On the other hand, there is a promise of untapped potential which could be interesting but involves a risk and more hard work. A choice must be made whether to take up the new challenge or stay with the safely tried and tested.

Student comments

ALEX (34) *This card reminds me of when I had finished my degree and was considering continuing with my studies. Although I had achieved a lot, I knew there was still a lot more I could do, and I had a sense of being between two options. One represented a safe choice of continuing to study, while the other option was a job offer in Africa which sounded exciting but was also very unstable. In the end I continued to study and am glad about it in one way, but I often wonder what would have happened had I taken the other route.*

SUSAN (51) *I associate this card with a decision I had to make when in my late teens. I was working as a secretary in a prestigious company where I was in line to become personal assistant to the managing director. I was perfectly happy but then a friend offered me the chance to be a freelance assistant on a photo shoot, which entailed three weeks of travel to the Far East. I asked my company for leave but they refused, so I gave in my notice and started a short career travelling as a photographer's assistant.*

These examples show possible options that this card could represent. The tarot will not say which way you 'should' go; it can only reveal the dilemma and invite you to think about the decision and its consequences.

NAME

DATE

PLACE

TIME

Colouring exercise
As you choose your colours for this card, feel the difference in choice between something tried and tested and something unknown. Half of the card symbolizes something established, while the other half is new. Which side draws you?

Personal association
Think about a time in your life when you had to make a decision such as the one implied in the Seven of Pentacles. Try to remember how you felt about it.

What this image means in my life _____

_____

_____

_____

Readings in which it was significant _____

_____

_____

_____

See Reading Record Sheet of _____

EIGHT *of* CUPS

Eight is the number of death and rebirth. Combined with the watery Cups it points to endings in the sphere of the emotions or relationships. The Eight of Cups shows a man turning away from eight neatly stacked cups, indicating that although effort has been invested in the display, it is not enough to keep him there. The moon is in its final waning phase, symbolizing something coming to its natural end.

Within a reading

The Eight of Cups suggests that something which has been the subject of careful attention is no longer satisfying or has outlived its time. It can be hard to reject something that has been a significant part of one's life, yet sometimes it is inevitable. When the Eight of Cups appears in a reading it symbolizes such a time.

Student comments

JAMES (33) *This card makes me think of an ending I experienced in a relationship when I realized that my girlfriend wasn't in love with me and I could do nothing except give up on her. I had tried to make things different but nothing worked. It was* hard to give up as I really did care, and I didn't want to face the truth. The image on the Eight of Cups of the hooded man walking towards the barren mountains reminds me of how bleak I felt when I had to face life without her.

SUSAN (51) *I can identify similar feelings when I ended a relationship I was involved in before I met my husband. I was young and in love with a man who was much older than me. I adored him and did everything I could to appear mature and sophisticated, which is what I thought he wanted. I gave up most of my friends and social circle, as he found them too young and boring, and generally tried to behave as if I was older than I was. I put a lot of effort into the relationship but it just wasn't working. Eventually I plucked up the courage to leave. Although it felt devastating, I knew it was the right thing to do.*

These examples both show that effort cannot change everything and sometimes the only action possible is to give up. There are times for striving and other times when the only solution is abandoning a situation. The Eight of Cups represents the latter.

NAME

DATE

PLACE

TIME

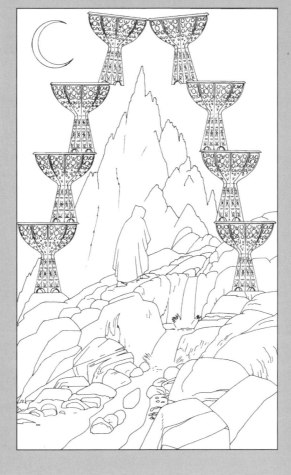

Colouring exercise
Choose colours to reflect
the serious mood of the
Eight of Cups, bearing in
mind that new beginnings
always follow endings.

Personal association
Try to match your own
experience to this card,
thinking of a time when
you had to give up on
something you had
wanted badly in the
sphere of relationships.

What this image means in my life ⎯⎯⎯⎯⎯⎯⎯⎯⎯⎯⎯⎯⎯⎯⎯⎯⎯⎯⎯⎯⎯⎯⎯

Readings in which it was significant ⎯⎯⎯⎯⎯⎯⎯⎯⎯⎯⎯⎯⎯⎯⎯⎯⎯⎯⎯⎯⎯

See Reading Record Sheet of ⎯⎯⎯⎯⎯⎯⎯⎯⎯⎯⎯⎯⎯⎯⎯⎯⎯⎯⎯⎯⎯⎯⎯⎯⎯

EIGHT *of* WANDS

When the number Eight combines with the fiery imagination of the Wands, a very different picture to the soulful Eight of Cups emerges. The number of regeneration works with the element of fire to produce many ideas and positive energy. A man firing arrows into the distance symbolizes a great time for action and initiative. This card marks a period of excitement and activity.

EIGHT *of* WANDS

Within a reading

The Eight of Wands shows a desire for expansion and inspiration. It indicates a period of activity when everything runs smoothly. It is a good time for travel, for getting projects off the ground and for action, not contemplation. Ideas are prolific and find their way to realization, rather than remaining interesting thoughts.

Student comments

ALEX (34) *This card makes me think of the sense of triumph I felt when I first got the amazing news that a publisher would take my novel. I had been working with many stops and starts, and many false hopes and rejections, so when the project eventually got the go-ahead it felt that things* were going my way at last. *The feeling of potential success was amazing. From being a nobody, facing continual rejection, things suddenly changed: editors were interested in working on the book and marketing was being put in place. Following a period of nothing, the gears changed and I was suddenly thrown into a world of activity.*

SUSAN (51) *This card reminds me of the period of activity we experienced when we ran a guesthouse. Having worked hard to decorate and furnish everything, there was a period of waiting for guests. Luckily, our very first visitors wrote a wonderful article about us, which brought a sudden flood of guests. Everything started moving at a fast pace. The large, empty house was suddenly full of people. The telephone rang constantly and we forgot what it was like to sleep for a more than a few hours at a time. It was exhilarating and we thoroughly enjoyed that time, even though it eventually got too much and we sold up.*

Alex and Susan both describe experiences of sudden success and the attendant activity, which correspond well with the Eight of Wands.

NAME

DATE

PLACE

TIME

Colouring exercise
This card is one of action
and adventure, so let your
choice of colours reflect
this optimistic mood.

Personal association
Remember your own times
of triumph and think of
situations where you felt
things were moving
forward for you.

What this image means in my life _____

_____

_____

_____

Readings in which it was significant _____

_____

_____

_____

See Reading Record Sheet of _____

EIGHT *of* SWORDS

Eight is the number of death and rebirth. Combined with the often difficult suit of Swords, it produces a somewhat uncomfortable situation. The woman is blindfolded and bound, surrounded by swords. However, the ropes only affect the upper half of her body, showing she is free to walk. Her hands are tied but not tightly, so it is clear that she could release herself from the restriction. The swords do not actually imprison her; they merely impede her progress.

EIGHT *of* SWORDS

wedding because I suspected my husband was being unfaithful. He promised me he wasn't, and plans for a big wedding went ahead. I did not want to cancel it, yet my doubts continued. I felt that whatever decision I made at the time would be the wrong one. In the end I chose to go ahead with the wedding and we ended up parting several years later. Looking back, however, I am glad I took the path I did because we have a wonderful daughter and grandson. They make everything truly worthwhile, no matter how difficult other aspects of my life have been.

Within a reading

The Eight of Swords symbolizes certain restrictions and difficulties. It shows that, while times are not easy, they are not impossibly hard either. Responsibility must be taken in order to change things. Perhaps the most difficult aspect of this card is deciding which direction to take out of an awkward situation.

Student comments

GERALDINE (62) *I associate this card with the period before I got married. Although I was in love, I was having doubts about going through with the*

SUSAN (51) *The Eight of Swords reminds me of the dilemma my husband and I had to face about how to manage our finances when he lost his job. One option was to sell our house and buy something smaller, a huge wrench as it was a beautiful family home. The other was to trust that he would find work so we could pay the mortgage again. In the end we decided to take in lodgers to pay the mortgage until my husband found work, which he did eventually.*

The Eight of Swords suggests a time when difficult decisions have to be taken with no guarantee of how things will turn out.

NAME

PLACE

DATE

TIME

Colouring exercise
Think of colours that might reflect the sort of difficulties suggested by the Eight of Swords. Remember the trouble is not insurmountable. Think of times in your life that remind you of something similar.

Personal association
Continue to think about situations that seemed insoluble and remember how you managed them.

What this image means in my life _____

Readings in which it was significant _____

See Reading Record Sheet of _____

EIGHT *of* PENTACLES

This card combines the number of regeneration with the earthy element of the Pentacles, resulting in an image of an apprentice. Also known as the card of talent, the Eight of Pentacles combines the notion of rebirth in the Eight with undertaking study or training with a view to earning money from it. The figure shown in the card image is dressed in work clothes and is certainly a 'hands-on' craftsman who is still in the process of learning his trade.

EIGHT *of* PENTACLES

Learning has none of the dreary connotations of study, which it did in childhood. I actually like doing my homework, and the course reading is a pleasure rather than a boring slog. How much it is due to my age or the subject, I don't know, but I love the experience now.

ALEX (34) *I associate this card with art history, which is one of my new areas of interest. My study of tarot sparked an interest in the imagery of the oldest decks and in Renaissance art. I did a tour of Italy and fell in love with the art and architecture. Since then I have taken a few courses on the subject. Not only does it tie in well with the tarot but I find all the related subjects continue to fire my imagination.*

Within a reading

This card can signify a mature student, as it suggests the kind of energy and interest experienced by those who actively want to find new work, or retrain in a specific field. It suggests enjoyment and appreciation of the process, a different flavour from school study, which is obligatory and has little to do with personal will or choice.

GERALDINE (62) *I feel that learning the tarot at my age and stage in life fits this card very well. I enjoy the classes and the learning process so much that I don't feel as if this is hard work at all.*

These associations with the Eight of Pentacles confirm this card's sense of interest in learning and achieving levels of competency for its own sake. Making a living out of that field of interest is almost incidental compared to the personal satisfaction obtained from the actual study itself. This kind of dedication and fascination in a subject is more common in mature students, where freedom of choice exists.

NAME

PLACE

DATE

TIME

Colouring exercise
Choose earthy colours
that reflect the solid,
enduring energy of the
Pentacles.

Personal association
Think of any situation in
your own life that reflects
this card's essence. Try to
get a personal feel for the
card, which is the best way
to make the card and its
meaning your own.

What this image means in my life

Readings in which it was significant

See Reading Record Sheet of

NINE *of* CUPS

Nine is the number of penultimate completion. Combined with the watery element of the Cups, its image suggests pleasure. A table decked with fruit and wine symbolizes physical gratification, while a couple embracing reflects the sensual delight associated with this card.

Within a reading

The Nine of Cups is traditionally connected with love, romance, sensuality and the joy that comes from feeling in harmony with another person. There are peak times in life when everything seems perfect, even if it is only for a little while. Moments like these are reflected by the Nine of Cups.

Student comments

SUSAN (51) *Thinking about the Nine of Cups takes me back to being in love with being in love in my early teens. I was on a family holiday in France, longing for a boyfriend, when I noticed a handsome French boy on the beach. I saw him every day but we were both too shy to speak until the last day of the holiday. When we finally spoke we got on really well and went for a walk on the*

NINE *of* CUPS

beach alone, which at the time seemed incredibly romantic to me. As we watched the sun go down over the water, he put his arm around me and kissed me – my first kiss – and it was a magic moment I thought I would remember forever. And I guess that's true, because I have just remembered it now after all these years!

JAMES (33) *My Nine of Cups moment was quite recent when I proposed to my fiancée. I wanted it to be a memorable occasion so I booked our favourite restaurant and ordered a dozen red roses before we arrived. I asked her to marry me (luckily she accepted) and I signalled to the waiter, who brought over the roses and a bottle of champagne. It was wonderfully romantic – perhaps really corny, but we both loved it. I know that marriage itself is not just one long romance so I am keen to create some special moments to get us through the grey times.*

It is true that peak moments can sustain us when things are hard, so they are not only nice but also necessary. The Nine of Cups is all about enjoying the dream for as long as it lasts.

NAME

PLACE

DATE

TIME

Colouring exercise
As you colour in the image, imagine what your own perfect moment was like. Remember that experiences described in each of the tarot cards are both archetypal and individual.

Personal association
Think of the associations and memories that this card conjures up for you personally.

What this image means in my life _____

_____

_____

_____

Readings in which it was significant _____

_____

_____

_____

See Reading Record Sheet of _____

NINE *of* WANDS

The fiery imagination of the Wands combined with the number Nine shows a final struggle before victory can be achieved. In the image the figure is fully engaged in the process, gripping his wand fiercely as he faces his opponent. Behind him, eight wands signify what he has already won and is fighting to protect. The bandage on his head reveals that the struggle is hard, but he does not give up.

Within a reading

The Nine of Wands describes a struggle, possibly relating to creative or artistic matters that have reached a critical moment. It requires utter dedication to succeed. Even though you may feel exhausted, there is strength in reserve.

Student comments

JAMES (33) *The Nine of Wands makes me think of when I had to use up every ounce of fighting spirit when working on an important project with a tight deadline. I had spent a whole weekend working on it at home on my computer and was nearly finished when the computer crashed before I saved it all. It was a truly awful moment. My first impulse was to leave the country, but failing that I realized I had no choice but to start again. With the aid of black coffee I worked solidly through the night and finally finished it. Looking back, I don't know how I did it. It was as if there was strength in reserve that I didn't know I had, yet it came through for me when I really needed it.*

CARA (24) *I associate this card with a nightmare drive I did on my own on the way home from staying in France with friends. A friend was supposed to drive back to England with me but couldn't come at the last moment. As a relatively inexperienced driver, the idea of a long drive alone on foreign motorways was not appealing but I had no choice. The situation got even worse when a storm blew up and soon I was battling through heavy rain and wind. The conditions were nightmarish. I was tired and terrified but there was nowhere safe to stop. I had to keep driving and concentrating, refusing to let my fear get the better of me. When I finally arrived, shaking with exhaustion, I was hardly able to believe I had managed.*

Cara and James both give clear examples of strength in reserve. The fact that they had to keep going or go under fuelled their desire to succeed, and that is typical of the Nine of Wands.

NAME

DATE

PLACE

TIME

Colouring exercise
As you colour in this card, choose colours that conjure up a sense of strength in reserve, identifying with the man in the image as he faces the opposition.

Personal association
Try to relate an experience of your own to this card. Use the students' examples to help call to mind your own memories.

What this image means in my life _____

_____

_____

_____

Readings in which it was significant _____

_____

_____

See Reading Record Sheet of _____

NINE *of* SWORDS

The number Nine combines with the airy element connected with the Swords to produce an image of sorrow. Nine swords are suspended over the weeping figure, and, although they do not harm her directly, they act as a threat, which evokes fear and anxiety.

Within a reading

The Nine of Pentacles is an image of disaster or doom which is often not founded on anything real but is nevertheless disturbing. It suggests a time of anxiety or doubt, or possibly a difficult decision to make which can cause pain, but the fear is worse than the reality.

Student comments

CARA (24) *This card reminds me of a horrible time when my father was taken ill and we didn't know what was wrong. He was in hospital for several days having tests, and those anxious days waiting for news were spent with my mother, brother and sister. Our fear led us to prepare for the worst. The image of the sleepless woman reminds me of how anxious we all were until we discovered that his condition, although serious, was not cancer*

NINE *of* SWORDS

or worse, and that he was beginning to respond well to his treatment. He ended up making a full recovery but it was a very unsettling time for us all.

SUSAN (51) *I remember an occasion, which sums up the Nine of Swords for me, when my eldest daughter was travelling in the Far East. She called to ask for more money for unexpected expenses and promised to phone us back the next day. However, she didn't call back for five days, which was out of character, during which time we had no way of getting in touch with her. By the time we heard from her I was beside myself with worry, images of disastrous scenarios flashing through my mind. It was such a relief to know she was safe after all, but I will not forget those five anxious days in a hurry.*

These examples describe the feeling of fear, which is awful, and, although there may be nothing real to suggest the fear is valid, we do not stop worrying. Instead we project our worst fears and nightmares right into the vacuum of the unknown. The Nine of Swords is more about the fear of impending doom than any real disaster.

NAME

PLACE

DATE

TIME

Colouring exercise
When colouring this image, think of occasions when you have been worried or concerned about something that didn't happen.

Personal association
Call to mind as many personal situations that relate to this card as possible. Reflect on the difference between fear and reality.

What this image means in my life _____

_____

_____

_____

Readings in which it was significant _____

_____

_____

_____

See Reading Record Sheet of _____

NINE *of* PENTACLES

The number Nine works with the earthy element of the Pentacles to produce an image of material security and earthly achievement. A richly dressed woman stands alone in a fertile vineyard in the grounds of a distant castle. The vines are lush and ripe, symbolizing that care has been taken to bring them to fruition, while the woman's elegant attire suggests material comfort and success.

NINE *of* PENTACLES

Within a reading

The Nine of Pentacles suggests peaceful enjoyment of the fruits of one's labours. The earthy nature of the card suggests material contentment and satisfaction. Out of all the elements, earth seems the most capable of feeling satisfied when a goal has been reached, without the urge to find another goal immediately.

Student comments

GERALDINE (62) *I feel as if I am in a Nine of Pentacles phase at the moment. I am really enjoying not having to work hard to make money, as I sold my gardening business profitably and can easily live off that income. My daughter is financially independent so I only have myself to consider and I don't have extravagant desires. I can, for the first time in my life, do pretty much what I want. I love my studies, I have my own little house and garden to tend to, which gives me pleasure, and I can make plenty of time for my grandson. I feel truly fortunate.*

ALEX (34) *I associate this card with getting royalty statements for the sale of my books. Whenever the cheque comes in I feel as if it is a bonus, as I am effectively getting money for work I've already done. The hard work is getting the books published. Once that's done, provided they stay in print, I keep getting rewarded, even though I haven't done anything new to earn the money. I associate this nice feeling with the Nine of Pentacles.*

These examples refer to a sense of satisfaction experienced after receiving financial recognition for past efforts. In Geraldine's case, the sale of her business enabled her to pursue another interest without fear of financial insecurity, while Alex experienced his royalties as a bonus. Both express a sense of contentment with their rewards.

NAME

DATE

PLACE

TIME

Colouring exercise
As you colour this image, consider the symbols of the earth's bounty and choose colours you feel express them appropriately.

Personal association
Think of situations from your own life which might relate to the message of the Nine of Pentacles. See if any of your own experiences match those of the students.

What this image means in my life _____

_____

_____

_____

Readings in which it was significant _____

_____

_____

_____

See Reading Record Sheet of _____

TEN *of* CUPS

Ten is the number of completion. In the watery element of Cups it relates to emotional ease. The image is of a family group, one member standing for each of the elements, suggesting a balance between all four. Although the image is one of family life, the happiness it represents is not always connected with families. The image is one of satisfaction rather than the ecstasy or bliss of the Nine of Cups.

Within a reading

The Ten of Cups reflects a state of contentment that has a sense of permanence. It is connected with a capacity to love, a generous spirit and the ability to give freely without counting the cost. This card also suggests a sense of appreciation and gratitude for love given and received.

Student comments

CARA (24) *I associate the Ten of Cups with a recent family occasion. To celebrate their silver wedding anniversary, my parents chose to take the whole family on a special holiday instead of throwing a party. The holiday turned out to be a great success. Our parents have always shown us – and each other – real kindness and generosity. This has paid off in the fact that we all really like each other and actually wanted to spend a week together. It felt like a positive testament to family life.*

SUSAN (51) *The Ten of Cups makes me think of family life, particularly my daughter's recent wedding. It turned out to be the kind of occasion we really treasured, not overly hyped-up but loving and friendly. My husband and I felt that our efforts had not been in vain. We have had our share of difficulties in our family and marriage, so it was good to have a positive affirmation in seeing our daughter so happy.*

Both these examples focus on positive family events, which is an obvious and traditional expression of the Ten of Cups. Although this card does not always focus exclusively on families, it does suggest a sense of permanence and contentment in emotional relationships.

NAME

DATE

PLACE

TIME

Colouring exercise
Choose colours you feel are harmonious and call to mind a sense of stability and contentment.

Personal association
See if you can relate this card's meaning to events in your own life. The more you allow yourself to think about such matters, the clearer the message this card reveals will be.

What this image means in my life _____

_____

_____

_____

Readings in which it was significant _____

_____

_____

_____

See Reading Record Sheet of _____

TEN *of* WANDS

The Ten of Wands graphically depicts an image of burden. The completion implied by the number Ten results in creative desires being overwhelmed; the imagination seems crushed by material concerns. The usually creative, spirited energy of the fiery Wands is stifled in the number Ten, resulting in oppression.

Within a reading

The oppression indicated by the Ten of Wands may be self-imposed. The fact that the burden is being borne voluntarily – it appears the figure in the image has chosen to carry the burden – suggests a possible solution can be found.

Student comments

GERALDINE (62) *This card makes me think of when I decided to sell my gardening business. I had been getting steadily more successful as the business grew. It had got to the stage where I had so much work I needed to employ people to do the physical labour. I ended up spending most of my time doing paperwork and quotes but not much gardening work, which was the aspect I liked best. The administration had begun to overwhelm me.*

TEN *of* WANDS

Curiously, it never occurred to me that I could change the situation until a friend said simply, 'Why not sell?' It was such an easy solution, but I hadn't thought of it until that moment.

This is a perfect example of how we get so used to difficulties that we don't think about changing things, even though we can. The figure on the Ten of Wands could put down his burden, yet he continues to struggle on.

CARA (24) *The Ten of Wands reminds me of my first year at university when I signed up to act in quite a serious capacity as representative to several clubs and social events. They were really fun projects and I wanted to do them all. The problem was I had severely underestimated how much time they would all take and how much energy I would need for them and for my own work. I ended up feeling as though I was drowning in everything I had taken on, and I was forced to cut back heavily on my commitments the following year.*

Cara's example highlights the enthusiastic influence of the Wands, which manifests as the desire to be creative, yet limits must be set if the result is not to be burnout.

NAME

DATE

PLACE

TIME

Colouring exercise
As you colour this image, allow yourself to identify with the figure on the card. Imagine you are carrying that bundle of wands and think about how you would manage it.

Personal association
Think about your own experience of taking on too much and not being able to manage it all, and how you resolved the situation.

What this image means in my life ⸺

Readings in which it was significant ⸺

See Reading Record Sheet of ⸺

TEN *of* SWORDS

The Ten of Swords is a graphic image of an ending. Ten swords pierce the back of a recumbent figure, yet dawn is breaking on the horizon. The Ten of Swords certainly suggests that the old order is changing, but in the distance the gathering light gradually pushes back the darkness with the message that the changes might be for the best. The butterfly is a symbol of transformation, so despite its gloomy image the Ten of Swords suggests a sense of clearing the ground for something new.

TEN *of* SWORDS

dear friend of mine. Nevertheless, I couldn't help thinking deep down that at last I could move on because the situation had ultimately come out in the open. It had been hidden, but not very well, for some time, which actually caused far more pain and tension than the final resolution.

The Ten of Swords often brings out something that has been hidden. James associates this card with learning the truth about something he had suspected. While the truth may be painful, it usually turns out to be preferable to a lie.

Within a reading

This card heralds a shift of perception and consciousness. It suggests a moment of catharsis, a death/rebirth situation. Something needs to die in order for something new to grow.

Student comments

JAMES (33) *The Ten of Swords calls to mind the way I felt after the ending of a love affair which meant a lot to me. I was doubly devastated because, in good cliché style, my girlfriend left me for a very*

ALEX (34) *The Ten of Swords reminds me of moving from America, where I had lived for most of my childhood, back to England. I was really happy in the US, which I thought of as home, so saying goodbye to friends, school and familiar surroundings was hard. I returned to a country that was called 'home' but which I hardly knew at all. I felt bereft and desolate for the first few months in England. However, in time I began to appreciate living in a country I knew was really 'home', where I was not known as 'the English kid'. I felt the benefit of extended family and we put down roots.*

NAME

PLACE

DATE

TIME

Colouring exercise
Use your own choice of
colours for this image to
conjure up how you feel
about the Ten of Swords.

Personal association
Reflect on situations of
endings in your own life.
Think of times when you
have needed to change for
a variety of reasons, and
consider both the positive
and negative aspects of
change.

What this image means in my life _____

_____

_____

_____

Readings in which it was significant _____

_____

_____

_____

See Reading Record Sheet of _____

TEN *of* PENTACLES

The Ten of Pentacles portrays a picture of family solidity and security. The old man, young woman and child in the grounds of a fine castle represent an image of permanence within changing cycles. The castle could symbolize material benefits passed down from generation to generation. This legacy could also be seen in less obvious gifts such as healthy genes, intelligence and beauty.

TEN *of* PENTACLES

Within a reading

The Ten, number of completion, comes to its natural conclusion in the earthy suit of Pentacles. There is a sense of permanence achieved partly through effort and hard work, and partly through good fortune. In a reading, the Ten of Pentacles indicates a materially settled way of life which may include property sale or purchase. It can also refer to traditional values being established.

Student comments

SUSAN (51) *I think of this card in connection with the legacy left by my father-in-law. He left us enough money to secure our family home as well as help* the children through higher education. He died after we had resolved a number of financial issues ourselves, but the money he left certainly helped take the pressure off long-term worries. We wanted to be able to leave our home to the children to ease financial burdens for them later in life, and it was important to give them the benefit of a good education. The inheritance helped us achieve those aims.

Susan sees the passing on of good fortune – which the Ten of Pentacles often symbolizes – in terms of inherited money, although it can also mean the inheritance of other things, as illustrated by James's example below.

JAMES (33) *This card is relevant to me at the moment as my fiancée and I are trying to sell my flat so we can buy our first house together before we get married. We plan to have children as soon as possible, so it feels like an important first step to secure a material base from which to grow a family. I like the sense of creating a permanent place from which we can pass on our love to our children.*

James relates the Ten of Pentacles to his wish to pass good feelings and love to his future family.

NAME

PLACE

DATE

TIME

Colouring exercise
As you colour this image, choose colours that reflect something solid and permanent.

Personal association
Use the student comments to start your train of association with the Ten of Pentacles.

What this image means in my life _____

_____

_____

_____

Readings in which it was significant _____

_____

_____

_____

See Reading Record Sheet of _____

PAGE *of* CUPS

The Pages are traditionally connected with messengers. They bring news of a potential event, which is why they are also associated with children. The Cups are linked with water and emotions, and the Page of Cups depicts a gentle child standing by a pool of water, symbolizing his feeling nature. He holds the golden cup in both hands, showing he takes the matter of his feeling life seriously, as he carefully watches a fish emerging. The fish represents his inner self, the part that is not easy to know – like fish, feelings are always moving and changing direction. As a messenger, the Page of Cups brings new understandings with regard to the world of emotions, which may involve self-love or love for others. As with all the Pages, the new beginnings this card refers to are fragile and easily crushed.

PAGE *of* CUPS

Within a reading

When this card appears it hints at changes in the emotional life. On a literal level it can bring news of the birth of a child, or it could symbolize the birth of new feelings.

Student comments

GERALDINE (62) *I associate the Page of Cups with the gradual restoration of hurt feelings after my painful divorce. I was profoundly saddened when my marriage failed; my husband was unfaithful to me, something I had feared for years and finally had to face. It took a long while to stop feeling bitter, but after a period of isolation I gradually started to expand my social life. Eventually I met a lovely man who was interested in me. I lowered my defences slowly and dared to feel love again. It was a slow process as I found it difficult to be trusting after my previous experience, but finally a relationship grew, which has now developed into something real. Although I don't want to marry again, my current relationship has proved more loving and satisfying than my marriage ever was.*

The Page of Cups can offer the possibility of a change of feelings, new feelings emerging or a broken heart being mended. The Pages are depicted as children because they represent their suit or element in potential. In the case of the Cups, it is the feelings that are in nascent form.

NAME

PLACE

DATE

TIME

Colouring exercise
Take the opportunity to understand the Page of Cups as you work on the image, choosing the colours that best reflect your understanding of the card.

Personal association
Think of circumstances and experiences in your life that best correspond to the Page of Cups. As usual, you might find it interesting to talk to others about their experiences.

What this image means in my life _____

_____

_____

_____

Readings in which it was significant _____

_____

_____

_____

See Reading Record Sheet of _____

PAGE *of* WANDS

The Page of Wands shows a young boy dressed in a tunic covered in suns and salamanders, symbols of fire, looking into the distance as if surveying the possibilities for future action. His wand is tilted towards the left of the image, the side of creativity, but he holds it in his right hand, the side of action. This suggests his desire for creativity is not merely a passing fancy but will soon be followed up with action. Traditionally, the role of Page was as an aide to someone of higher status, with a view to moving up the ranks. The Page of Wands therefore suggests that a tiny creative spark may grow into something grand and serious, given the right time and conditions. The Pages represent small beginnings that can evolve into something substantial.

PAGE *of* WANDS

Within a reading

The Page of Wands points to the beginning of a creative idea which, if carefully nurtured, may evolve into greater inspiration. As is the case with everything in embryonic form, great care must be taken to ensure its survival.

Student comments

ALEX (34) *I think the Page of Wands' energy was at work when I got the idea for my second novel. It was one of those odd occasions when I was bored on a Saturday afternoon and began flicking idly through the television channels. I came upon an old film about King Arthur and Guinevere. I began to watch it out of sheer boredom but afterwards I was aware that an idea for a story was beginning to form. As I thought about the legend, an idea began to unfold seemingly all on its own. Although my novel is not remotely based on the legend, a tiny fragment of the story was a seed for the plot. It is fun to trace the origin of an idea, which I often associate with the Page of Wands.*

The Pages act as ushers who guide a process into activity, just as a little lighted match tossed into a heap of dry wood may be enough to start a huge fire. As Alex says, it is good fun following ideas to see how and where they start, and which ideas 'take off' and which fizzle out.

NAME

DATE

PLACE

TIME

Colouring exercise
Choose your own colours to reflect the fiery, creative nature of the Wands. The traditional colours for fire are red, yellow and orange, but you should choose the colours that bring the card alive for you.

Personal association
Try to trace the origin of creative ideas or projects you have been involved in. Think about how you respond to initial sparks of inspiration. Do you tend to encourage or squash such notions in yourself?

What this image means in my life _____

_____

_____

_____

Readings in which it was significant _____

_____

_____

_____

See Reading Record Sheet of _____

PAGE *of* SWORDS

The Swords reflect the element of air or, as a psychological function, the capacity to think. While fire represents imaginative and creative inspiration, air symbolizes thought, which is logical and rational. The Page of Swords wears a tunic decorated with butterflies, symbolizing air, while the different types of birds flying overhead reflect the mind's ability to rise high above an earthy reality to explore many different concepts. The element of air most clearly reflects mankind's unique capacity for logical thought, and is the element that most obviously separates humans from the animal kingdom. The Pages all reflect something in nascent form, so combined with the air this card signifies new ideas and the emergence of different ways of thinking.

PAGE *of* SWORDS

Within a reading

The Page of Swords suggests a curious mind which can be used positively or negatively. There is great potential for original thinking, trivia such as gossip or even deceit. It is possible to resolve the conflicts often associated with Swords through honest communication.

Student comments

CARA (24) *The Pages make me think of children, so one of my associations with the Page of Swords is with schoolchildren and the way they learn though chatter and gossip. I vividly remember the endless hours we used to spend at school chatting. Mostly we would talk simply for the sake of talking. We would spend hours debating the most insignificant topics like whether straight hair was better than curly. When I hear my teenage siblings talking now, I am amazed and amused at how they love to talk for the sake of it. They are much less concerned with the content of their communication than with the actual process itself. Sometimes it is clear they are waiting to speak and not listening at all. It is also interesting to observe this dispassionately as they learn how to test ideas, often for their own benefit. For me, the Page of Swords is about experimenting and practising with ideas in order to figure out what is really important.*

The Page of Swords indicates the beginnings of mental processes. The double-edged sword reminds us that new ideas and thoughts may grow into something significant or simply fade away.

NAME

DATE

PLACE

TIME

Colouring exercise
As you choose colours
for this image, notice the
movement in the Page of
Swords, which is more
obvious than in the other
Page cards. This indicates
the mental activity the
Swords represent.

Personal association
Think up your own
associations to the Page
of Swords. See how your
experiences of new ideas
and ways of thinking
correspond to this card.

What this image means in my life ⎯⎯⎯⎯⎯⎯⎯⎯⎯⎯⎯⎯⎯⎯⎯⎯⎯⎯⎯⎯⎯⎯⎯⎯⎯

Readings in which it was significant ⎯⎯⎯⎯⎯⎯⎯⎯⎯⎯⎯⎯⎯⎯⎯⎯⎯⎯⎯⎯⎯⎯

See Reading Record Sheet of ⎯⎯⎯⎯⎯⎯⎯⎯⎯⎯⎯⎯⎯⎯⎯⎯⎯⎯⎯⎯⎯⎯⎯⎯⎯

PAGE *of* PENTACLES

The Page of Pentacles stands in a newly ploughed field wearing farming clothes in the earthy colours of brown and green. Solid and down-to-earth in appearance, he seems serious and cautious. He holds his pentacle carefully in both hands, as if to protect it from harm. The Pages all stand for early new beginnings, and the combination of the Page with the earthy Pentacles suggests a new start in practical matters. The Pentacles describe material achievements, so the image of seedlings is apt for the Page, as he represents something small and tender which must be carefully nurtured in order to flourish.

PAGE *of* PENTACLES

Within a reading

The Page of Pentacles suggests new beginnings in the material realm which need cherishing in the early stages of development. This card can indicate the start of a venture, perhaps a new business or project which may herald financial reward. Nevertheless, nothing will grow successfully without the necessary investment of careful hard work in the early stages.

Student comments

SUSAN (51) *The Page of Pentacles reminds me of my neighbour, who is a very good cook. She needed extra work, but with family commitments found it hard to find a 'proper job'. She decided to use her skills and organize cooking lessons for schoolchildren in her kitchen. She started out with a little group made up mostly from her children's friends, so at first it was a tiny enterprise making small amounts of money. However, she gradually became more popular and was asked to do more courses, even to run cooking parties for children's birthdays. From a small beginning she has built up a thriving business and now employs people to help her. Being self-employed, she is able to choose her hours to suit the family, and at the same time she is growing a good little business.*

Susan's story is a good illustration of the kind of slow yet solid growth that is particularly associated with the Pentacles in general and the Page of Pentacles especially. The Page of Pentacles implies a gradual build-up of resources through constant effort and application to a project. The suit of Pentacles describes the patience and hard work involved, but also the rewards such efforts bring.

NAME

PLACE

DATE

TIME

Colouring exercise
Although the colours that generally describe the earthy suits are brown and green, feel free to use your own colours to reflect how you relate to the Page of Pentacles.

Personal association
Match the meaning of this card to your own experiences. Think of situations in your life, or even the lives of your friends as Susan did, which call to mind the energy of the Page of Pentacles.

What this image means in my life ⎯⎯⎯⎯⎯⎯⎯⎯⎯⎯

Readings in which it was significant ⎯⎯⎯⎯⎯⎯⎯⎯⎯⎯

See Reading Record Sheet of ⎯⎯⎯⎯⎯⎯⎯⎯⎯⎯

KNIGHT *of* CUPS

The Knights all signify movement and action, for their astrological quality is mutable, meaning volatile and changeable. Pisces, the mutable water sign of the zodiac, is linked with the world of feelings. Its symbol is two fish swimming in opposite directions. Small fish decorate the Knight's tunic, connecting him with Pisces. The Knight of Cups is known as the lover, whose quest is for emotional unity. Traditionally this card represents an idealist and a seeker of perfection, mostly in the area of relationships. He is unashamedly in love with love, whether of a romantic or a spiritual nature.

KNIGHT *of* CUPS

Within a reading

The Knight of Cups indicates romance and a proposal of some kind. This could be a proposal of marriage or an artistic proposition. He may also represent a rival in love. However, the key point connected with the appearance of the Knight of Cups is that love is an important issue, whether it be romantic, platonic or spiritual.

Student comments

JAMES (33) *I associate the energy of the Knight of Cups with a dear Piscean girlfriend whose driving* force in life is the search for love. *While she is not a girlfriend in the romantic sense, we have been best friends for many years. Her main quest in life is searching for the perfect relationship. In a chameleon-like way that I believe is typical of Pisces, she tries to adapt herself to fit in with every man she falls in love with. She is essentially fairly bohemian by nature, but when she unexpectedly fell in love with an accountant she cut her hair into a neat bob and dressed the part in little black dresses and court shoes. That relationship ended and she fell in love with an outdoor type, so she changed her image and lifestyle again, this time buying her clothes from army stores. Not long after that she fell for a Frenchman, moved to France and when I last saw her she looked like a model for* Vogue *magazine. It was fascinating to observe the way she transformed herself into the image she thought her lovers wanted her to have, as though she really didn't mind who she was as long as she was both in love and loved.*

Although not all Pisceans will go to such lengths, Pisces is a sign known for its capacity to transform or sacrifice itself for love. The connection between Pisces and the Knight of Cups is the quest for an ideal relationship and the longing for love.

NAME

PLACE

DATE

TIME

Colouring exercise
As you colour this image, think about what the Knight of Cups means to you. Use colours to reflect the harmony, peace and love represented by this card.

Personal association
Consider your own associations to this card and to the sign of Pisces. Think about the various kinds of love connected with the card, from romantic to spiritual.

What this image means in my life ⎯⎯⎯⎯⎯⎯⎯⎯⎯⎯⎯⎯⎯⎯⎯⎯

Readings in which it was significant ⎯⎯⎯⎯⎯⎯⎯⎯⎯⎯⎯⎯⎯⎯

See Reading Record Sheet of ⎯⎯⎯⎯⎯⎯⎯⎯⎯⎯⎯⎯⎯⎯⎯⎯

KNIGHT *of* WANDS

The Knight of Wands depicts a young man on a galloping horse with fiery images of suns and salamanders decorating his cloak, and with a large feather symbolizing truth adorning his helmet. The mutable fire sign symbolized by the Knight of Wands is Sagittarius, the sign connected with a quest for meaning and knowledge. In the distance stand two pyramids, symbolizing mystery and ancient wisdom, qualities also linked with Sagittarius. The Knight of Wands is traditionally known as a card of change, which could refer to residence, country or career. The powerful imagination associated with the element of fire is directed towards a desire to discover new horizons. For Sagittarians, the joy is in the quest. They do not care for power; they are much more interested in a search for meaning.

KNIGHT *of* WANDS

Within a reading

The Knight of Wands symbolizes travel. These journeys may be literal, spiritual or psychological. The card may point to a change of residence or even a move abroad. He may also represent an enthusiastic person or a longing for personal expansion.

Student comments

ALEX (34) *I am Sagittarius and identify to a large extent with many aspects of the Knight of Wands. I am certainly more interested in discovering what things mean than I am in collecting or owning things. I guess you could say I have a philosophical nature, which I believe is supposed to fit Sagittarius, though I prefer journeys of the mind and imagination to physical travel. I am certainly restless; once I have discovered how something works or what it means I want to move on to discover more, or even to another adventure or puzzle. I maintain that the disadvantage of the mutable signs is their lack of patience and commitment. I personally find absolute commitment to a person, place or thing very difficult. I hate to be limited or to feel fenced in, which is probably why I am still not in a long-term relationship. I like the idea of intimacy, but whenever I get close to someone I get nervous and bolt. The image of the Knight of Wands, who sits so joyfully on his energetically galloping horse, is a real favourite of mine. I feel he is a kindred spirit!*

Alex's description of himself reflected in the Knight of Wands seems apt. He captures the themes of the Knight of Wands, which are freedom, love of life and adventure, and the joy of the quest rather than the prize.

NAME

DATE

PLACE

TIME

Colouring exercise
Choose colours you feel
are appropriate to call
to mind the spirit of the
Knight of Wands. Allow
your imagination free rein
to think about the card's
meaning.

Personal association
Think about the sign of
Sagittarius and those you
know born under it. See
how well they fit the
description of the Knight
of Wands.

What this image means in my life _____

_____

_____

_____

Readings in which it was significant _____

_____

_____

_____

See Reading Record Sheet of _____

KNIGHT *of* SWORDS

The Knight of Swords is on horseback, charging at top speed yet heading directly into the wind. Opposition of a mental kind is symbolized by the wind, the kind of intellectual challenge most air signs enjoy. The Knight of Swords represents the mutable quality of air in the zodiac sign of Gemini. The court cards may represent people in your life or aspects of yourself that you wish to cultivate. The Knight of Swords may mean that a lively, chatty, witty Gemini type comes into your life, or it might imply that you wish to develop some of those qualities in yourself. While Sagittarius is keen on the big picture, Gemini is fascinated by small details. Gemini loves to gossip, network, make connections between one thing and another and then move on. It is known as the butterfly of the zodiac, flitting from one flower to another. The Knight of Swords symbolizes similar energy entering your life, turning it around and then moving on. He is not boring, although he can be exhausting and frustrating to those who prefer a quiet life.

KNIGHT *of* SWORDS

Within a reading

The Knight of Swords represents a sudden change. Although this may be disruptive, it is necessary as the current situation may be getting stagnant.

Student comments

CARA (24) *One of my sisters is Gemini and she never stops talking. She is really articulate, great with words; she can write essays, letters, poetry and even songs with amazing ease. She strikes me as being a typical Gemini in that she is always coming up with new ideas, finds it remarkably easy to communicate with others and is never lost for words. She is great at networking, good at getting ideas off the ground among her friends and is at the centre of the gossip-web. She always seems to know what's going on in many different spheres of life. She is definitely on the easily bored side; she tends to take up interests quickly, get terribly enthusiastic about them and then drop them equally quickly, but she is so bubbly and such good fun that everyone tends to overlook her shortcomings. Her energy makes me think of the Knight of Swords.*

The Knight of Swords symbolizes an ambivalent character in many ways. He represents twists and turns which change things around, but in a necessary way. He has a reputation for being disruptive, yet he is also interesting and charismatic and manages to offset chaos with charm.

NAME

DATE

PLACE

TIME

Colouring exercise
As you colour the image, think about the element of air. Pay attention to the symbols on the image, as they all help you remember key points about the card when doing readings.

Personal association
Think of those you know born under the sign of Gemini and compare them with the energy of the Knight of Swords.

What this image means in my life

Readings in which it was significant

See Reading Record Sheet of

KNIGHT *of* PENTACLES

The Knight of Pentacles rides a farm horse which, unlike the other Knights' horses, is designed for work rather than pleasure. His horse stands still in a ploughed field, its bridle and blanket decorated with acorn leaves to symbolize the Pentacles' earthy connection. Knights represent the mutable quality, which in the element of earth is the industrious, versatile zodiac sign of Virgo. A hard-working sign in pursuit of perfection, Virgo is not averse to paying attention to detail. It is the sign of service, and gets satisfaction from a job well done. The Knight of Pentacles is traditionally known as an honest hard-worker who will achieve or create without drama or fuss. All the Knights are on a quest, and the Knight of Pentacles' goal is to achieve the necessary order to create a perfectly functioning world. This involves being critical because a quest for perfection cannot include sloppiness. Virgoans have a propensity to criticize themselves and others, and as a result tend to be high achievers.

KNIGHT *of* PENTACLES

Within a reading

The Knight of Pentacles ensures that important matters will ultimately reach a sound conclusion. The qualities of perseverance and patience can be well used and will come from within or from a person entering your life.

Student comments

SUSAN (51) *My husband is Virgo and he is certainly very determined when it comes to getting a job done properly. No matter what the task, mental or physical, he will research the subject thoroughly. He is never afraid to put himself through the necessary paces to complete the task in hand. I admire the determined way he devotes himself to an important but dull task with as much resolve as to something he finds interesting. I always skip boring details, which often means disappointing results, while my husband never lets himself off the hook like that. Consequently he ends up with successes on his hands, no matter how minor. He is utterly reliable, which is a quality I associate with the Knight of Pentacles, whose stable image on a stationary horse makes me think of safety and security.*

The earthy Knight of Pentacles reflects the natural cycles of the earth. Virgo calls to mind the orderliness of nature and the way in which all the earth's inhabitants are organized and co-ordinated. The sun passes through the sign of Virgo at harvest time; as soon as the harvest is gathered it is time to prepare the fields for planting again, and so the cycle repeats.

NAME

PLACE

DATE

TIME

Colouring exercise
Concentrate on the earthy element of the suit of Pentacles when working on this image. Reflect on nature's cycles and choose colours that mirror your thoughts.

Personal association
Match up the meaning of this card with your own understanding of Virgo.

What this image means in my life _____

_____

_____

_____

Readings in which it was significant _____

_____

_____

_____

See Reading Record Sheet of _____

QUEEN *of* CUPS

The Queen of Cups is portrayed as a beautiful woman seated on a throne made up of an oyster shell, mermaids and dolphins, all watery images of emotional depths. The Queens represent the fixed quality, which is stable and contained, seeking to preserve and nurture. Astrologically, the fixed water sign is Scorpio. The Queen of Cups is traditionally known as 'the beloved' in the way the Knight of Cups is 'the one who loves'. She is mysterious and charismatic. Like many Scorpios, she is not easy to get to know, Scorpio being the most secretive, private sign of the zodiac. The Queen of Cups is very sensitive to her own feeling world. She is portrayed staring intently at her reflection in the cup, as she continues her quest for self-understanding.

QUEEN *of* CUPS

Within a reading

As is true of all the court cards, the Queen of Cups can manifest herself in many different ways. She may enter your life as a mysterious, fascinating person or a beloved, or she may herald the emergence of feelings you wish to develop.

Student comments

GERALDINE (62) *My daughter is a Scorpio and she certainly reminds me of the Queen of Cups. She is intuitive, intense and extremely emotionally demanding. She is prepared to give herself one hundred per cent to those she loves but she expects the same commitment from others. She has a profound understanding of emotions and is not afraid of knowing the truth – no matter how ugly or unpleasant it may be, she would prefer it to any kind of lie. It makes her a very uncompromising person to live with. As a child she was not easy, nor was she ever dull. In adolescence I noticed that the boys would find her fascinating, not because she flirted like other girls, but because she seemed rather self-possessed and aloof in some way. Although she is demanding, she isn't needy, and this quality seems to attract others to her. She is quite content to be alone, which she would much prefer to being with those she considers superficial or frivolous.*

Geraldine's description of Scorpio and the Queen of Cups seems fitting, as the card and sign are primarily concerned with understanding the mysterious, elusive depths of feelings and the unconscious mind.

NAME

DATE

PLACE

TIME

Colouring exercise
When colouring this image, let your imagination loose on watery symbols such as the ocean, mermaids and fish, choosing your colours accordingly.

Personal association
Think about what the Queen of Cups means in your life and whether you can identify with her, either in yourself or in others you know.

What this image means in my life _____

_____

_____

_____

Readings in which it was significant _____

_____

_____

_____

See Reading Record Sheet of _____

QUEEN *of* WANDS

The Queen of Wands appears warm in contrast to the cool Queen of Cups. She is seated on a golden throne decorated not only with the familiar fire symbols of salamanders and flames, but also with lions, the symbol of the fixed fire sign Leo. The Queen holds a sunflower, a solar plant, in her left hand, reflecting her creativity, while in the right hand of action she holds her wand of authority. She is able to command a position of respect in the world as well as sustain relationships and family life,

QUEEN *of* WANDS

symbolized by the cat at her feet. The suit of Wands is fiery, enthusiastic and creative, yet, unlike the Knight and King, the Queen will not gamble unless she knows she will win. The fixed quality of the sign works through the element of fire by combining nurture and intuition to good effect. The lion is king of the animal world, and Leos tend to see themselves as royal. They are at their most magnanimous and generous when performing before an audience, as they feel loved and fulfilled when acclaimed or adored by others.

Within a reading

The Queen of Wands suggests that a person who possesses her qualities of warmth, imagination and *joie de vivre* may enter your life, or that you are in need of developing such attributes within.

Student comments

JAMES (33) *One of my best friends is a Leo and I can certainly connect him with the energy of the Queen of Wands. He fits the bill nicely by being an actor, so he is true to type in that respect, but he is also a loyal and kind friend. Married with a small child, he is able to devote his abundant strength and energy to his family as well as to his career. His extravagant warmth and generosity make him popular, and he is at his best when he has people admiring him. He is an affectionate, amusing father and a loyal husband, although he isn't good about being ignored or sharing the limelight. In general, however, because he's so charming and charismatic, he manages to get away with prima donna outbursts better than most.*

James's friend sounds like a true Leo, with characteristics appropriately reflected in the Queen of Wands. Her image reveals royalty and authority, symbolized by her throne and wand of power, yet her flower and cat soften any harsh edges. The fixed quality of Leo means that creative ideas and inspiration can be harnessed so that projects are likely to come to fruition.

NAME

DATE

PLACE

TIME

Colouring exercise
Choose colours you feel
best reflect the energies
of the Queen of Wands.
Think about her best and
worst qualities.

Personal association
Associate the Queen of
Wands with someone you
know, or see whether you
can find aspects of her in
yourself.

What this image means in my life _____

_____

_____

_____

Readings in which it was significant _____

_____

_____

_____

See Reading Record Sheet of _____

QUEEN *of* SWORDS

The Queen of Swords is portrayed so that only one side of her is visible. She sits straight, alert, even on edge, as if she is prepared for whatever hand life deals her. Traditionally, the Queen of Swords is connected with disappointment or sorrow, and if we look more deeply into her connection with the fixed air sign of Aquarius we might understand why. Aquarius, sign of humanity, brotherhood and high ideals, is primarily concerned with visions of improving the world. Air is connected with thinking, and is forever seeking a better, fairer and more civilized way for the human race to evolve. It is not difficult to like Aquarians because they are civilized, charming and easy to be with. The problem is that human beings are also blessed with irrational feelings, which sometimes complicate the progress of the intellect. Aquarians are often disappointed when relationships fail to live up to their high ideals and expectations.

Within a reading

The Queen of Swords may suggest despondency or sorrow, often due to unrealistic expectations. She seeks a perfect world, so when she discovers clay feet she finds it more

QUEEN *of* SWORDS

disappointing than most. You may need to examine your dreams and ideals to be sure they are realistic.

Student comments

CARA (24) *I shared a house at university with an Aquarian. At first I thought she was the most easy-going, charming person imaginable, yet when I got to know her better I saw a surprisingly stubborn, inflexible side. She had certain notions of what was right for the world, and lectured us for hours on human rights and world poverty, but was rather bad at remembering to do her own dishes! She fell in and out of love equally swiftly as her partners inevitably failed to live up to her expectations. Her sparky originality made her exciting to be around; she was both stimulating and annoying at the same time.*

Fixed signs tend to dislike too much change. The combination of fixity and the element of air – the element that seeks change – is a complex one. It can result in a certain narrowness, which is unexpected in an original, free-thinking sign such as Aquarius. The Queen of Swords is similarly complex. She is a powerful figure who is prepared to fight for her lofty beliefs, but at the same time she resists change and is inclined to see the emotional world as inferior to that of the intellect.

NAME

DATE

PLACE

TIME

Colouring exercise
As you colour this image, think about the variations this card reveals. None of the tarot images are simple, but in many ways the Queen of Swords is more complex than most.

Personal association
Think about what this image means for you personally. Allow yourself to reflect on the various sides of this interesting card.

What this image means in my life _____

_____

_____

_____

Readings in which it was significant _____

_____

_____

_____

See Reading Record Sheet of _____

QUEEN *of* PENTACLES

The Queen of Pentacles sits in a natural flower garden with a rabbit, symbol of fertility, by her throne. She holds a pentacle, symbol of nature's magic. The throne is decorated with bulls' heads, connecting the image with Taurus, the sign of fixed earth. The Queen's cloak is embroidered with red roses, symbolizing love, and her robes are green to connect her with Venus, the goddess of love and beauty and ruling planet of Taurus. The earthy sign of Taurus is associated with a love of beauty and quality in the material world such as good food and wine, fine clothes and harmonious surroundings. At home in her body, the Queen of Pentacles is concerned with physical health and well-being and is unashamed about spending time and money on herself, which she considers to be essential rather than a luxury.

QUEEN *of* PENTACLES

Within a reading

The Queen of Pentacles suggests that a self-sufficient, generous and hard-working individual may enter your life. This card can also imply that it is appropriate for you to attend to your physical needs and sensual desires.

Student comments

CARA (24) *I am a Taurus and I relate very easily to the Queen of Pentacles. I am happy as long as my surroundings are pleasing and comfortable; the material side of life is important to me. I like beautiful fabrics, soft furnishings and tasteful, harmonious colour schemes, and feel quite unhappy in ugly places. I hate activities like camping as they often involve being cramped, damp or cold. I definitely aspire to being a five-star-hotel sort of girl, even though I don't have anywhere near that sort of money yet! I also dislike too much change; I tend to stay in relationships for long periods and many of my friends are life-long. I loathe conflict and am happy to work hard as long as I can see the results. My goals in life are not hugely ambitious: I would prefer a happy marriage with a family to being fantastically successful in a glittering career.*

Cara's description is an apt one. The Queen of Pentacles is content as long as she is comfortable and in a peaceful relationship in which she can enjoy the so-called simple pleasures of life. She is not enormously ambitious in a worldly sense, although she is fiercely protective of anything she is responsible for, be it work or family.

NAME

PLACE

DATE

TIME

Colouring exercise
As you colour in this image, think about nature, its cycles and the safety found in their constant rhythm, which is similar to that of the element of earth.

Personal association
Think about what the image of the Queen of Pentacles means in your life. Think about how well or otherwise you relate to what she represents.

What this image means in my life _____

_____

_____

_____

Readings in which it was significant _____

_____

_____

_____

See Reading Record Sheet of _____

KING *of* CUPS

The Kings are characterized by the cardinal quality, providing the necessary action and energy when initiating new projects. In the watery Cups, where feelings dominate, this action is often connected with relationships. Traditionally, the King of Cups is linked with the church or the healing professions, perhaps because they are both concerned with people and their feelings, whether spiritual or physical. The cardinal water sign is Cancer. The paradox with Cancer and the King of Cups is that the realm of water and feelings is feminine, while the cardinal qualities are masculine. The image shows this uneasy combination by portraying the King with dry feet yet surrounded by water. Around his neck he wears a golden fish on a chain, as if to suggest his feelings are safely in check. The King of Cups longs to be emotional and empathize with others, yet he finds it difficult to trust and surrender to the world of feelings. The Queen of Cups happily merges with the ocean, while the King of Cups keeps his feet dry.

KING *of* CUPS

Within a reading

The King of Cups suggests that someone may enter your life who understands the world of feelings. This may refer to the start of an emotional relationship. Alternatively, it may mean a professional who will help you. The King of Cups can also indicate that you will be playing that role in someone else's life.

Student comments

ALEX (34) *My father was Cancer. He was a doctor so he fits the description of the King of Cups quite well. He was an excellent physician, well-loved by his patients, but I think his calm and kind professional front hid his frightened, reserved side, which was vulnerable to being hurt. He was often in danger of getting tangled up with his patients' lives and problems. As a father he was always there for his family but he would never break down and let anyone really take care of him. Even at the end of his life he minimized his own pain, never complaining, and accepting suffering stoically.*

The King of Cups is a difficult image to understand because it is so complex. He is a genuinely sensitive soul who possesses the gift of understanding others and communicating that to good effect. However, when it comes to giving of himself he is much more guarded. He wants to trust but does not dare let go completely.

NAME

DATE

PLACE

TIME

Colouring exercise
When colouring this image, pay attention to the various symbolic details. Notice the carved fish on his throne and the leaping fish of his imagination, which is safely out of his view.

Personal association
Match your own insights and experiences to the King of Cups as you continue to build up your understanding of its deeper meanings.

What this image means in my life _____

_____

_____

Readings in which it was significant _____

_____

_____

See Reading Record Sheet of _____

KING *of* WANDS

The King of Wands is connected with the dynamic, active energy of the cardinal sign of fire, which corresponds with Aries. His clothes and throne are decorated with salamanders and suns, symbols of fire, and the golden rams represent Aries. He appears to be leaning forward as if anxious to be on his way, a typical posture for this active King. The sign of Aries corresponds with spring and is bursting with energy, enthusiasm and desire for new initiatives. Like the other fire signs, Aries is creative and imaginative as well as impulsive, restless and eager for adventure. Ariens are born leaders, gifted with the warmth and eagerness to inspire others to get involved in whatever new ideas they dream up. The King of Wands is a risk-taker and a gambler; even if he loses he takes the best out of the situation and turns it into a win.

Within a reading

The King of Wands suggests a warm, fiery individual is set to enter your life, generating changes and setting the scene for something new. If this card is not representing a person, it suggests that the time is ripe for developing these qualities within you.

Student comments

GERALDINE (62) *My partner is an Aries and he is certainly similar to the King of Wands. To him, having fun is a serious business. He tries to ignore the downsides of life and concentrate on having adventures. As a true optimist he is inclined to overlook the negative and concentrate firmly on the positive, even though his life hasn't always been easy. He is spontaneous, impulsive and endlessly enthusiastic, which is both wonderful and exhausting. I find his 'everything is possible' attitude annoying at times because, as a Capricorn, I am inclined to be more solemn about life and take things very seriously. In my experience, Aries can be a selfish and egotistical sign, but never deliberately malicious or unkind, and that counts for a great deal with me.*

Geraldine's description of the King of Wands is fitting both for the card and the sign of Aries. Arien exuberance is fun but it can be overbearing for more sensitive, introverted souls. However, without its enthusiastic optimism the world would certainly be a sadder, less colourful place.

NAME

DATE

PLACE

TIME

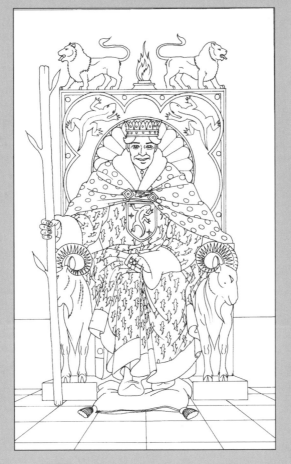

Colouring exercise
When colouring in this image, think of Ariens you know and love, or hate. See how they correspond to the King of Wands.

Personal association
Try to think of personal relationships you have had with Ariens and what you have found when working with the King of Wands in readings.

What this image means in my life _____

_____

_____

_____

Readings in which it was significant _____

_____

_____

_____

See Reading Record Sheet of _____

KING *of* SWORDS

The King of Swords is con-nected with Libra, the cardi-nal air sign, which reflects the dynamic, initiating, active aspect of the element. The King wears a purple cloak, the colour of wisdom. Overhead fly two birds, a symbol of the duality of Libra, which desires equilibrium. Traditionally, the King of Swords is associated with the legal profession. Libra is a sign committed to using the mind to find fair and bal-anced solutions to all life's opposites. The King of Swords is a serious figure who metes out justice in accordance with the laws that society, rather than nature, deems to be fair. All the air signs appreciate civilized manners and dislike discourteous, aggressive behav-iour, but Libra desires harmony above all else. The element of air is the one furthest away from the instinctual animal kingdom, and the development of intellectual prowess and skill is highly prized.

KING *of* SWORDS

Within a reading

The King of Swords suggests it is time to start developing your mental skills and intel-lectual prowess in new ways. It can also mean that a figure of authority, perhaps connected with the legal profession, may enter your life.

Student comments

SUSAN (51) *My daughter is Libra and I see plenty in common between her and the King of Swords. She has a finely tuned sense of justice and always used to sort out play-ground disputes at school. She con-tinues on the path of peacemaker and diplomat, working in a human resources team where she is well-respected, firm but fair, and man-ages to use an 'iron fist in a velvet glove' to good effect. She has a good, although not particularly academic, mind and is very organized and able to plan and execute ideas effi-ciently. My feeling about the King of Swords is that he loves truth and justice and is prepared to work hard for it. He has a certain cool-ness of character but is trustworthy and dependable, which are qualities my daughter also possesses. She is a leader but in a quiet way. People follow her with-out always realizing it because her power is wielded unobtrusively. She hates aggressive conflicts or ugly scenes, and any battles she fights will be done through the intellect, not in a flesh-and-blood way.*

Susan's description of the King of Swords is an apt one as she has captured beautifully the subtle strength in the airy sign of Libra. Just because the King of Swords dislikes bloody battles does not mean he is a wimp; he goes about his battles using mental, not physical, weapons.

NAME

PLACE

DATE

TIME

Colouring exercise
Think carefully about
which colours you feel
best reflect this image of
intellectual strength and
prowess.

Personal association
As you consider this
card, match up your own
associations with it that
you have come across in
your readings. Think, too,
about your experience
of the sign of Libra.

What this image means in my life _____

_____

_____

_____

Readings in which it was significant _____

_____

_____

_____

See Reading Record Sheet of _____

KING *of* PENTACLES

The King of Pentacles represents the dynamic and initiating dimension of earth in the cardinal sign of Capricorn. The armrests of his throne are carved with the heads of mountain goats, symbolic of Capricorn. The connection between the King of Pentacles and the earth is reflected in the luxuriant vines around him, while a majestic castle symbolizes his desire for material status. Capricorn is an ambitious sign with high ideals and aspirations for power and worldly achievement. The King of Pentacles is an image of material wealth and a strong desire to reach positions of power and authority. He is generous to those he considers deserving. Once he fulfils his desired ambitions he is able to take pleasure in the results of his efforts. The King of Pentacles enjoys making money but most of all he enjoys the power that material possessions can bring, as society's recognition of his standing is most important to him.

KING *of* PENTACLES

Within a reading

The King of Pentacles suggests it is time for worldly challenges to be faced. He may appear in your life as a powerful figure who influences your material position in the world, or he may point out that you must take on these challenges yourself.

Student comments

JAMES (33) *My boss is Capricorn and I associate him with the King of Pentacles. Although he is a successful businessman, he is elegant and gentlemanly in the way he goes about making money, though I am sure he must have a ruthless streak to be as successful as he is. Nevertheless, he presents himself as reserved, almost modest; nothing about him is flamboyant or extravagant. Everything he possesses seems to be of the highest quality but he doesn't make a big deal out of it. He is concerned about his image so never makes a fool of himself by losing his temper. In fact, the nearest he gets to being rude is to be bitingly sarcastic. Of course, I don't know the real man at all, but he is certainly a figure of respect in our company and we all do our best to stay on the right side of him.*

James's description of the King of Pentacles and his experience of a Capricorn employer is a good illustration of this card. The King of Pentacles is an image of material concerns and a desire to acquire status and recognition through wealth.

NAME

DATE

PLACE

TIME

Colouring exercise
Use colours that best reflect the earthy qualities of this card for you. As always, pay attention to the symbolic detail of the image as this helps jog the memory when doing readings.

Personal association
Try to think of your own associations with the King of Pentacles. Perhaps you can identify with him personally, or can see his qualities in friends or family members.

What this image means in my life ———————————————————

———————————————————————————————

———————————————————————————————

———————————————————————————————

Readings in which it was significant ————————————————

———————————————————————————————

———————————————————————————————

———————————————————————————————

See Reading Record Sheet of ——————————————————————

THE FOOL

The traditional image of The Fool is a youth because he represents new beginnings. He is about to walk off the edge of a precipice. This reminds us that anything new involves a risk because the territory to be explored is uncharted. In many decks, as in this one, an animal appears snapping at the young man's feet, as if to discourage him from making a mistake or dangerous move. The start of something new often brings fear as well as a sense of excited anticipation. However, the sun shining brightly ahead is a symbol of optimism. A butterfly – symbol of the soul's ability to transform – flutters overhead, indicating a quest for personal knowledge and expansion.

THE FOOL

Within a reading

The Fool stands for change, new beginnings and the risks involved in facing the unknown with an open mind.

Student comments

CARA (24) *I associate The Fool with each of the big developmental stages of my life so far, starting first with school. I can remember clearly the excitement of going to school and being delighted with my uniform and satchel. I felt very grown up until*

I got to the gates and had to let go of my mother's hand. Then I felt petrified, but the desire to grow up and be big somehow helped propel me through the door. I think I felt the same when I moved to secondary school, and certainly when I left home and went to university, and finally into my own flat. With each move I was aware that I had outgrown my surroundings and it was time to move on, and on each occasion I was in touch with very mixed feelings of excitement tinged with fear of the unknown.

Cara's thoughts on The Fool offer a clear illustration about how it feels to change. The Fool represents a stage in life when the past starts to become restrictive, even imprisoning, while the future offers a chance to expand and grow. The 'unknown' always before us, offering its pot luck of possibilities, could be wonderful, average or dreadful, yet we cannot find out what awaits us without taking the risk and making a move. The Fool represents our individual need to change, grow and expand. He stands for a new cycle about to begin, whether it be at work or home, in relationships or beliefs. The Fool does not always stand for traditional changes; he is often an image of the unpredictable and even unwise, yet his longing for growth tends to obliterate doubt.

NAME

DATE

PLACE

TIME

Colouring exercise
As you colour in The Fool, imagine you are in his shoes, about to walk off the edge of a cliff. How does it feel? Use colours that reflect these feelings.

Personal association
Think of your own experiences of new beginnings. Recall and record those that capture the spirit of The Fool.

What this image means in my life _____

_____

_____

_____

Readings in which it was significant _____

_____

_____

_____

See Reading Record Sheet of _____

THE MAGICIAN

The Magician appears here, as in the majority of decks, with a table or altar in front of him, on which are displayed the emblems of the Minor Arcana. These emblems symbolize the four elements – water, fire, air and earth – and describe the various options available: the emotional Cups, the intuitive Wands, the logical Swords and the material Pentacles, respectively. The Magician acts as a catalyst, presenting us with opportunities that send us down unexpected paths. These can be strange coincidences or chance meetings, or even those experiences that we put down to 'being in the right place at the right time'. His colours are red and white, to symbolize a need to find a balance between earthly passions and spiritual aspirations. He stands with one hand pointing towards earth and the other towards the heavens, showing himself as a link connecting the two.

Within a reading

The Magician represents a new range of opportunities, options and choices, and signifies the necessary skills, talents and chances to explore them. It is a card of great energy and creativity.

THE MAGICIAN

Student comments

GERALDINE (62) *I think The Magician was at work in bringing me to study the tarot. In a carefree frame of mind while on holiday a year ago, I wandered into a little bookshop and started to browse absent-mindedly in the mystic section. I knew nothing about tarot and wasn't particularly interested in it, but for some reason I picked up a book on the subject and started to flick through. I quickly became fascinated, bought the book and that was where my tarot journey began, not very dramatically and quite unintentionally. It seemed to come along at just the right moment and opened up a new world filled with images, myths and symbols. This felt like The Magician at work to me.*

This is a lovely example of The Magician's energy acting as a prompt in a particular direction. It would seem that Geraldine was ready for something new, although she didn't know it consciously at the time she walked into the bookshop. The Magician presides over the strange 'coincidence' of picking up a book at random and finding it absorbing, but it was Geraldine's perseverance and commitment to her new subject that ensured its longevity. The Magician announces the arrival of opportunities and possibilities; it is up to us to make something of them.

NAME

DATE

PLACE

TIME

Colouring exercise
As you choose colours
for this card, consider the
various symbols for The
Magician that you could
use as memory aides
when doing readings.

Personal association
Think of any of your own
experiences that could
be connected with The
Magician. Perhaps you
could trace the way you
came to study tarot, using
the student comments as
a springboard for your
own associations.

What this image means in my life _____

_____

_____

_____

Readings in which it was significant _____

_____

_____

_____

See Reading Record Sheet of _____

THE HIGH PRIESTESS

The High Priestess used to be known as the female Pope, and in older decks is often depicted as a nun. Here she is pictured as a young woman in white, the colour of virginity and purity, symbolizing her unfulfilled potential. She is crowned with daisies, the flower of innocence, while on her lap she holds narcissi, flowers associated with death and rebirth. Behind her stand twin pillars, which represent the opposites of masculine and feminine, day and night, good and evil. Each pillar is topped with a crescent moon, symbolizing the beginning of a new cycle. The veil hanging between the pillars is decorated with pomegranates, the many-seeded fruit connected with fertility.

THE HIGH PRIESTESS

Within a reading

The High Priestess is connected with esoteric, secret matters. There is an emphasis on unseen potential, which needs to be brought to light gradually. The theme of this card is a gentle unfolding of inner understanding – spiritual, intuitive and emotional – just as a foetus slowly develops in the dark secrecy of the womb.

Student comments

ALEX (34) *I understand The High Priestess best when I am in the early stages of writing. I start to have vague notions, too tenuous to be called ideas, which I can't speak about to anyone. They feel too fragile and delicate to risk discussing, yet I know something is happening in the deepest recesses of my creative mind. I am nowhere near ready to put anything on paper. All the activity is going on inside and not all of it makes sense, but I do have a powerful feeling that something is going to come out of it. There is a strong intuitive sense that the process must be allowed to develop in its own time, although I can get impatient, even despairing, if it takes too long.*

Alex's experience is a good description of a process that matches the mood of The High Priestess. This card represents something in potential which must be allowed time and space to mature and evolve. It is feminine in its nature, thus it cannot be directed by the rational mind; rather it is guided by intuition or imagination.

NAME

PLACE

DATE

TIME

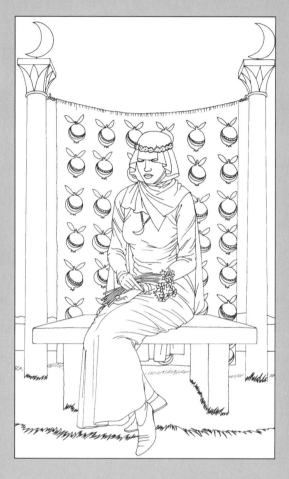

Colouring exercise
As you colour in this image, think about its connection with any process of gestation – literal or creative – using colours you feel are applicable.

Personal association
Try to link this card with any of your experiences of allowing something inside you to grow and develop. Choose a piece of music that stimulates your imaginative powers and use this as a theme for the card.

What this image means in my life _____

_____

_____

_____

Readings in which it was significant _____

_____

_____

_____

See Reading Record Sheet of _____

THE EMPRESS

The Empress is seated in a ripe cornfield, holding a sheaf of corn on her lap. At her feet the horn of plenty overflows with fruit, symbolizing the richness of earth's bounty. The Empress is a symbol of potential fulfilled and possibilities realized. She is the virginal High Priestess turned mother, traditionally depicted as a mature woman in a position of some authority. While she is often connected with maternal care, her nurturing is not limited to physical children. She symbolizes the care needed when raising any kind of child, whether it is a physical or a creative offspring. The poppy, flower of death, grows in the corner to remind us that anything living must eventually die. Her crown has twelve stars, representing the signs of the zodiac, reminding us that the yearly cycles of blossom, fruit, decay and death are in constant motion.

THE EMPRESS

Within a reading

The Empress suggests a period of fertility and abundance. This can operate on a number of different levels, relating to family relationships and children but also to all kinds of creative projects.

Student comments

SUSAN (51) *The Empress reminds me of all the relationships that exist within my family from my own mother, to my husband and children and eventually grandchildren. I am aware of the chain of nurture passing from generation to generation, and of the bittersweet aspects of mothering and being mothered. The death of my mother, whom I loved dearly, was a profound loss for me, and now I am in the process of witnessing my own children growing up and moving on into adult life. This is both painful and joyful, as I miss being a central figure in their lives yet I am proud and pleased for them. It is also providing a space for me to pursue other projects, which I find satisfying.*

Susan's associations to The Empress are close to the most traditional interpretations of the card, which relate to family life. However, The Empress presides over all manner of creativity, so the same emotions Susan describes apply to almost any creative project. A play, for example, is conceived in the imagination, brought to life in the script, performed in the theatre and finally taken off the stage. For the playwright, actors and producers, the same cycle of blossom, fruit, decay and death is evident.

NAME

DATE

PLACE

TIME

Colouring exercise
As you colour in the image, pay attention to the various symbols – such as the water as it falls into the river – suggesting the union of male and female to produce a child. Notice all the details and choose your own colours in response to the imagery.

Personal association
Think of your own associations in connection with mothering. Consider how you nurture and care for yourself, and think about how much of that is governed by your positive or negative experiences in childhood.

What this image means in my life ———————————————————

————————————————————————————————————

————————————————————————————————————

————————————————————————————————————

Readings in which it was significant ———————————————————

————————————————————————————————————

————————————————————————————————————

————————————————————————————————————

See Reading Record Sheet of ————————————————————————

THE EMPEROR

The Emperor is richly dressed in purple and red, the colours of wisdom, majesty and power. His fine throne is decorated with eagles, which are associated with royalty, as they fly higher and have keener eyesight than any other bird. The Empress is his female counterpart, representing feminine softness in her lush landscape, while The Emperor's terrain is the barren land of logic and discipline. As The Empress is mother, so The Emperor is father, the one who sows the divine seed which creates life.

THE EMPEROR

The Emperor's role is to bridge the gap between the family and the outside world. He engages in business, politics and world affairs, constantly seeking to create a better world for his children and fellow citizens. He wears the crown of authority and holds the orb and sceptre, symbolizing masculine potency and an understanding of the laws of the material world. Together, The Empress and Emperor represent the opposites of feminine and masculine forming a balanced whole.

Within a reading

The Emperor points towards success in a worldly sense, and to material ambition or achievement. He is often associated with concrete matters such as the buying of property, or with bringing ideas into some sort of reality.

Student comments

ALEX (34) *I identify The Emperor with all kinds of authority figures ranging from my father to various bosses and, more recently, my publishers. I think of The Emperor as a more objective figure than The Empress. She reminds me of my own mother, who is encouraging and sympathetic and tends to see the best in me, even when I don't always do a particularly good job. The Emperor, on the other hand, seems more like my father, who always encouraged high standards and would never make allowances just because I was his son. For me, The Emperor symbolizes a strong, effective figure who strives for the best for society. He is a powerful force working with the benefit of future generations in mind, prepared to take on the task of continually seeking to improve the world as a whole.*

Alex's view on The Emperor captures his essence well. The Emperor stands for action taken following a good idea. He is traditionally associated with the material or commercial world, where he is able to realize ambition in a concrete sense.

NAME

PLACE

DATE

TIME

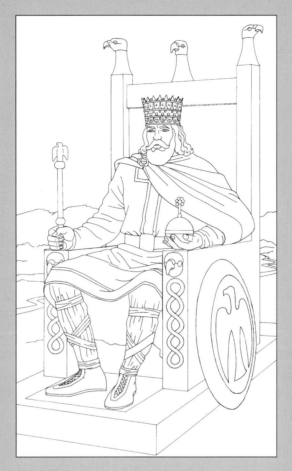

Colouring exercise
Choose colours you feel
are powerful and strong.
Think of your associations
with power – both positive
and negative – as you
work on this image.

Personal association
Think of your own
experiences that connect
with the meaning of The
Emperor. Are any of his
qualities ones that you
recognize in yourself or
do you see them only
in others?

What this image means in my life _____

_____

_____

_____

Readings in which it was significant _____

_____

_____

_____

See Reading Record Sheet of _____

THE HIEROPHANT

The Hierophant is portrayed in many older decks as a Christian priest. Here, however, he is depicted simply as a holy man, dressed in plain white robes to symbolize spiritual purity. His three-tiered crown represents body, mind and spirit. He does not symbolize any particular religion; his true essence is that of a spiritual guide. His chain with crossed keys symbolizes knowledge of good and evil, and The Hierophant himself acts as a balance between two pillars, which stand for all opposites.

THE HIEROPHANT

He is a symbol of the spiritual side of the masculine, just as The Emperor stands for the worldly side. While The Emperor acts as a guide on the practical, material journey through life, The Hierophant is a guide on the inner journey, unseen yet hugely important.

Within a reading

The Hierophant signifies the search for inner meaning and spiritual awareness. He stands for guidance on spiritual or emotional matters.

Student comments

ALEX (34) *This card makes me think of my psychotherapist. He has been a very important figure for me over the past few years, helping me to understand some fundamental truths about myself. Initially I sought help for a specific problem which I hoped would be easily solved. However, I soon became aware that the panic attacks I was experiencing were a symptom of other, more deep-rooted problems. As I began to attend to those issues, the panic attacks went away quite quickly. Nevertheless, I wanted to continue the exploration, which I am still doing. My therapist provides space for me to work on myself and acts as a guide on the inner journey, shedding light when I cannot see where I am going. On the outside I may not seem that different, but inside things feel a whole lot calmer.*

The Hierophant's energy is clearly reflected in Alex's experience of one kind of guide on the road to inner balance and integrity. The Hierophant may also appear as a teacher or a religious person. The main point is that he is connected with the search most of us wish to take for personal meaning and purpose in life. The Hierophant can also represent books that inspire us, symbolized by the open tome on his lap. The High Priestess contrasts with him in that her role is to intuit and feel her way through situations in accordance with the feminine principle, while The Hierophant wants to learn and consciously seeks answers in accordance with the masculine.

NAME

PLACE

DATE

TIME

Colouring exercise
As you colour this image, think about the differences between the masculine and feminine principles, not confusing them with male and female. Reflect on the spirit of The Hierophant and what he represents for you.

Personal association
Think of how this image works in your own life. Connect it with people, books or ideas that have changed your world-view. Think about your own quest for understanding and see how it is reflected in this card.

What this image means in my life

Readings in which it was significant

See Reading Record Sheet of

THE LOVERS

The card of The Lovers depicts a choice. In an image similar to that of many traditional decks, a young man stands uncertainly between two women, who both look to him for a decision. One woman is older and experienced, wearing red, the colour of sexual passion. The other woman is young and wears white, the colour of innocence. The man wears yellow, the colour of mental energy, which alerts us to the part the mind plays in the process of decision-making. Above him flies Cupid, the god of love, who likes to play games with human emotions. He may create havoc by firing either golden arrows of love or lead arrows of hate into an unsuspecting human heart.

THE LOVERS

Within a reading

Although The Lovers card immediately makes us think of love affairs because of its title, it really points to choice. A decision must be made. We must be aware of the consequences of our choice, whether or not it concerns romance.

Student comments

SUSAN (51) *The Lovers card makes me think of an important decision I made when I was in my early twenties. I was head over heels in love with a divorced man much older than me. He already had three children and didn't want to get married and have another family. This broke my heart so I decided to leave him. It was a hugely difficult step for me. In fact, I left the country because I couldn't trust myself to be anywhere near him. I established a new life abroad, and in time met a new man of my own age. I was just feeling settled when I received a letter from my old lover asking me to marry him. It took all my strength not to go running back, but after thinking about it long and hard I decided not to return.*

Susan's example of the conflict and uncertainty involved in making a major decision is an apt one. The main theme of The Lovers card is a need to make choices, and our best bet is to make them in as much of an informed way as possible. The tarot cannot make choices for us; it can only point out that a choice must be made and it is up to us to figure it out as best we can.

NAME

PLACE

DATE

TIME

Colouring exercise
As you choose colours to reflect how you feel about this card, consider also the dilemma of the young man as he chooses between the two women.

Personal association
Think of the various choices you have made in your life and how you feel about them now. Maybe you have to make one at the moment. If so, use the imagery in the card as a guide in the decision-making process.

What this image means in my life

Readings in which it was significant

See Reading Record Sheet of

THE CHARIOT

The Chariot is an image of a battlefield in which passions run high. The charioteer in a red cloak, the colour of desire, is desperately trying to control his two horses. One horse is black and the other is white, representing his opposing feelings, thoughts and desires. The symbol of a scorpion found on the charioteer's breastplate connects him with battles, as Mars, the god of war, is co-ruler of Scorpio. The Chariot's essence is the conflict and tension that opposites inevitably create. The opposing forces in human nature can be identified as the carnal and spiritual drives which, in a healthy psyche, are balanced. Managing internal conflict is an on-going struggle, because conflict is necessary to promote change and growth. Without any kind of friction, nothing would change and the result would be stagnation.

THE CHARIOT

Within a reading

The Chariot represents a struggle or conflict of interests, which can be played out either on an inner level, or between oneself and others. Victory follows a battle, but first the obstacles must be faced and difficulties overcome.

Student comments

GERALDINE (62) *I feel that The Chariot sums up my on-going struggle with my weight. I am always trying to lose weight or at best not to put any more on, but my desire for good food often gets the better of me. The two horses, for me, are images of my desire to eat and my desire to be slim, and those two are constantly having a battle inside me. Sometimes my greed gets the better of me, while at other times I manage to starve myself, and occasionally I reach the middle ground where I am able to eat, but not too much. I find maintaining the balance hard to achieve and I can identify this process with the charioteer's struggle to keep the two horses together.*

Geraldine appropriately describes the conflict between wanting two things that are mutually exclusive as a battle that neither side should win. The ideal place is, of course, the middle ground where both sides gain something and lose something, but it is a hard place to maintain. The Chariot is a passionate card and it requires courage to tackle instinctual desires and feelings.

NAME

PLACE

DATE

TIME

Colouring exercise
Choose colours that best conjure up a sense of conflict and struggle for you. Try to identify with the charioteer as his interests clash with those of his horses.

Personal association
Find a personal example of wanting two different things at the same time. How do you find a compromise, or do you let one side win over the other?

What this image means in my life _____

_____

_____

_____

Readings in which it was significant _____

_____

_____

_____

See Reading Record Sheet of _____

JUSTICE

Justice reveals an image of a woman holding a sword, which represents truth, and scales, symbolizing balance. Much of the symbolism in this card can be found in the colours. The woman wears a green dress, the colour of Venus, goddess of love. Her red cloak is the colour of Mars, god of war. The presence of both green and red suggests a balance between these opposing qualities. Her headdress is yellow, the colour of mental communication. The purple veil behind her is the colour of wisdom, and this links two pillars, representing the eternal opposites. To her left is the owl of wisdom, whose vision is so powerful that it can see in the dark. Justice seeks to attain the ideal of harmony through balancing the mind, and using the intellect to make unprejudiced and dispassionate decisions.

Within a reading

As Justice is connected with the intellect and the element of air, it suggests there is a need to weigh up situations impartially, in order to find fair and objective solutions. Sometimes this has to be done at the expense of emotions.

Student comments

JAMES (33) *I associate Justice with a search for righteousness and fairness using the intellect. I find discussions on the subject fascinating, since we are always searching for ideal situations where fairness and reason can prevail. But we also keep coming up against the other reality: that nature itself isn't fair – at least not in the way mankind uses the word. I like the idea that all could be treated with genuine equanimity, yet I see how impossible that is to achieve. Justice, taken to its extreme, might have no heart. To me, the Justice dilemma is described clearly by the image on the El Gran Tarot Esoterico deck, which shows King Solomon about to cut a baby in half to satisfy the demands of two mothers who laid claim to the infant. It would be fair for the two mothers to have half a baby each, but to kill an infant to achieve fairness would clearly be ridiculous.*

James's comments prompted a fruitful discussion about how Justice can be seen from several angles. One of Justice's key themes is cool calculation and reason, which may prevail at the expense of empathy and compassion. The card that follows Justice is Temperance, whose connection with the feeling element of water can mitigate Justice's tendency towards cold objectivity. The balanced mind needs to stand beside the balanced heart.

NAME

PLACE

DATE

TIME

Colouring exercise
As you colour the image, try to find appropriate shades to conjure up a sense of the Justice card. You can use similar colours to the ones described, or find other representations of your own.

Personal association
Try to find ways of matching your own experiences to the Justice card. It would be helpful and interesting to discuss the concepts with other people.

What this image means in my life _____

_____

_____

_____

Readings in which it was significant _____

_____

_____

_____

See Reading Record Sheet of _____

TEMPERANCE

The Temperance card portrays an angel carefully pouring liquid from a gold cup, symbolizing the masculine principle, into a silver one, representing the feminine. Gold is the colour of the sun and stands for the daytime world of the conscious mind, while silver is the colour of the moon, and stands for night-time and the unconscious. Together they form a balance, which is symbolized by the flow of water between one cup and the other. The angel stands with one foot in a pool of water, reflecting the feminine, while the other is on dry land, suggesting the masculine.

TEMPERANCE

Within a reading

Temperance stands for sharing, compromise and co-operation in relationships. It carries with it the connotation of successful, contented connections with others.

Student comments

JAMES (33) *The Temperance card has become especially important for my fiancée and I, as we have been consciously employing the techniques of co-operation and compromise in our relationship. We have been living together for nearly two years now and are due to get married in a few months'* *time. We discussed the principles of this card in terms of our communication and came up with jointly agreed rules. The golden one is always to talk about whatever is bothering us, no matter how difficult it might be. We have both had experiences of hiding things in other relationships and are determined not to let that happen this time. We try to balance out each other's moods; we share all the household tasks because we both know it can bring resentment when one person gets stuck with a grotty job. Some people say we haven't been together long enough to know whether we can keep it up for a lifetime but we certainly intend to try. I think the main thing is that we are aware of the need to compromise. As we both understand and use the tarot images, we have the image of Temperance pinned up on the fridge to act as a daily reminder.*

James and his fiancée have made a positive decision to use the energy of Temperance in a practical way in their relationship. The fact that they have pinned the image up in their kitchen is a particularly good idea because it acts as a constant reminder of what they are trying to achieve as a couple. Using the tarot in this everyday fashion can be very helpful, especially if both parties understand the symbols.

NAME

DATE

PLACE

TIME

Colouring exercise
As you colour this image, concentrate on the flow of water from one cup to the other. Notice the rainbow of hope in the background as the sun rises behind the twin mountain peaks, suggesting reconciliation between opposites.

Personal association
Think of how Temperance is, or indeed isn't, working in your own life at the moment. How does this card's meaning affect your daily life? Think of situations that call for co-operation or compromise and reflect on how you manage them.

What this image means in my life ⎯⎯⎯⎯⎯⎯⎯⎯⎯⎯⎯⎯⎯⎯⎯⎯

Readings in which it was significant ⎯⎯⎯⎯⎯⎯⎯⎯⎯⎯⎯⎯⎯⎯

See Reading Record Sheet of ⎯⎯⎯⎯⎯⎯⎯⎯⎯⎯⎯⎯⎯⎯⎯⎯

STRENGTH

The Strength card shows a young woman calming a large lion by forcing its powerful jaws open with her bare hands. Although unarmed and barefoot, symbolizing her external vulnerability, she remains undaunted and faces her opponent with courage. She does not wish to kill the lion; she is attempting to render him harmless so his power can be harnessed. The lion is a solar beast, symbolizing the masculine principle, while the maiden is dressed in white to reflect her connection with the moon and the feminine. She wears garlands of red roses and white lilies, which represent both passion and purity. The strength evident in this image is not physical, but is, rather, connected with self-discipline and struggles of an inner nature. The lion symbolizes the inner beast, or instinctual desire, which must be contained and disciplined for it to be truly effective.

STRENGTH

Within a reading

The Strength card suggests the possibility of achieving self-awareness, personal inner strength and determination, and the courage to take on the task of self-discipline.

Student comments

CARA (24) *Just now I associate the Strength card with a dance class I have recently started on Saturday mornings. It is something I really enjoy and want to do, but it starts early and involves a tedious journey. I hate getting up early on Saturdays, so on many mornings I have an internal battle between the part of myself that wants the enjoyment of the dance and the part that doesn't want the struggle of getting out of bed and going to class. The image of the woman struggling with the lion makes me think of my struggle with my undisciplined side, which threatens to take over from time to time. I think I will put the Strength card next to my alarm clock on Friday nights! I like the idea of using the imagery to enhance my daily life as it enlivens the meaning of the card in a really positive way.*

Cara and James have found ways to use the images of Strength and Temperance as memory aides to help them with their current individual concerns. The Major Arcana images are archetypal and will always be applicable in our lives in some way or another. Finding ways of making the images work in our daily lives as well as in readings for others can be a potent form of self-help.

NAME

DATE

PLACE

TIME

Colouring exercise
As you colour the image, think about current situations in your life that involve strength and personal courage. Try to reflect them in the colours you choose.

Personal association
Use the Strength card to help you envisage personal inner struggles. As you identify them, allow yourself to think about how you handle them.

What this image means in my life _____

_____

_____

_____

Readings in which it was significant _____

_____

_____

_____

See Reading Record Sheet of _____

THE HERMIT

The Hermit is an image of age, reflected by a grey-bearded man carrying a staff and lantern. The staff suggests he needs support, while the lantern is required to light the way as his twilight years approach. The snake accompanying him is a symbol of the continual process of transformation, as snakes naturally shed and renew their skins periodically throughout their lifetime. The Hermit stands for the passage of time. He can be likened to The Fool at the mid-point of his journey.

THE HERMIT

The older man is not as carefree as he was in his youth. Unlike The Fool, he now looks at the path ahead with care. He must rely on the light from his lamp as the sun has set.

Within a reading

The Hermit stands for a period of solitude and soul-searching. He represents patience, acceptance and tolerance of himself and others, the prizes of maturity.

Student comments

GERALDINE (62) *As the oldest member of the group I expect I am best qualified to talk about The Hermit. Funnily enough, the older I get, the more contented I become on an inner level. I don't like the physical side of old age much – the slowing down and getting wrinkly – but I do like the inner peace and tranquillity it brings. I no longer fear being alone; in fact, I find I am truly able to enjoy the experience. Now I relish pleasing myself and being selfish, which doesn't mean I wish to withdraw from social or family life at all. It's just that I don't feel a failure if I am not with other people all the time. I associate the sense of peaceful acceptance of my life with The Hermit. When I was younger I was constantly complaining about the shortcomings and disappointments of my life, and longing for things to be different. Now I see them all as part of my life's unique pattern and do not wish to change anything.*

Geraldine's description of The Hermit is lovely. It is a gentle card that offers a sense of the inevitable, which is not worth fighting against, but well worth working alongside. We must all age. Youth can never be reclaimed in a concrete sense. However, the benefits of wisdom, memory and patience are all qualities that can be positively distilled from the passage of time.

NAME

DATE

PLACE

TIME

Colouring exercise
Use the colouring exercise to focus your attention on the ageing process, with both its advantages and disadvantages.

Personal association
Think of your own experience of ageing. Think of yourself, your parents, your friends and your own circle and consider how those around you face the question of maturation.

What this image means in my life _____

_____

_____

_____

Readings in which it was significant _____

_____

_____

_____

See Reading Record Sheet of _____

THE WHEEL OF FORTUNE

The Wheel of Fortune suggests continual change. The imagery is similar to that of many old decks in which men's fortunes rise and fall according to the whim of the blind goddess Fortuna at the centre, who turns the wheel without knowing who will be affected. Fortune could rise like the man ascending. There may be triumph, symbolized by the crowned figure at the top of the wheel, or fortunes may fall, shown by the man going down. At the base of the wheel is a ragged man, who is without any fortune at all. The key point about this card is that no one can stay in one position forever. The wheel is always moving, as does each man's fortune.

THE WHEEL OF FORTUNE

Within a reading

The Wheel of Fortune signifies a new beginning, a new chapter opening or a new run of luck. The important thing is to remember that all runs of luck, whether good or bad, do eventually come to an end.

Student comments

SUSAN (51) *I find The Wheel of Fortune a fascinating card. Looking back over my life I can see the various turns of the wheel, which have taken me and my family through a great many phases. I feel I have loved and been happy, lost and been sad. Our family life has moved through financial success to ruin when my husband was made redundant, which felt like being at the base of the wheel. We then climbed back up to relative financial success, only to be cast down by problems with our son, who suffered from depression and caused us great anxiety. He has gradually recovered and the family had cause for great celebration at our daughter's wedding. However, I know now that life is constantly moving and we can never be complacent or depend on anything. I think it has the positive effect of making us more appreciative of all the good we do have while we have it; I take nothing for granted any more. I like this card because it tells a story of life in the truest way: nothing lasts and everything is valuable.*

The Wheel of Fortune is a fascinating card, as Susan rightly points out. Its message may seem simple yet it is extremely profound. It can have the effect of helping us focus on what is essential in the here-and-now, rather than projecting worries too far into the future. It tells us that the only thing we can safely count on is that life will continue to change, which means there is constancy within change.

NAME

PLACE

DATE

TIME

Colouring exercise
As you colour in the image, consider the cycles of birth, blossom, decay and death in The Wheel of Fortune.

Personal association
Try to find associations with times of gain and loss. Think about how you coped with both, perhaps at different times of your life.

What this image means in my life _____

_____

_____

_____

Readings in which it was significant _____

_____

_____

_____

See Reading Record Sheet of _____

THE HANGED MAN

The Hanged Man is an image associated with sacrifice. A man is suspended by his ankle, but although his position seems uncomfortable his expression is serene, not tortured, and his head is encircled with white light. The twelve branch stumps on the trees represent the signs of the zodiac. His feet are associated with Pisces, the twelfth sign. The sun passes through Pisces during March, the Christian period of Lent; it is during Lent that preparations are made to honour Christ's

THE HANGED MAN

sacrificial death, which was made so that humans could have everlasting life. Sacrifice means giving something up in order to gain something of greater value, and it is entirely voluntary. Here, the figure's hands are folded behind his back, revealing his commitment not to take action but to allow the sacrifice to go ahead.

Within a reading

In order to gain, something must first be relinquished yet the decision is voluntary. The Hanged Man is an image of conscious choice; there is no question of being forced into any decision. A sacrifice is made willingly, yet it involves an act of faith because there are no guarantees regarding the outcome.

Student comments

GERALDINE (62) *The Hanged Man calls to mind for me the kind of sacrifices I was glad to make for my daughter. When she was growing up I wanted her to have as many opportunities as possible. Being a single mother for many of those years, finances were tight so I had to work very hard to get the extra money needed in order to provide her with those things. Nevertheless, I was happy to make those sacrifices because it gave me pleasure to see her grow and flourish. I was aware that it was entirely my choice; she didn't need the music or the riding lessons, and it was certainly me who wanted her to have them. While she benefited from the extras, I enjoyed providing them.*

The notion of sacrifice can be seen in many ways. Geraldine talks about the sacrifices she made for her child. Others may be prepared to sacrifice luxuries for learning, or indeed vice versa. Whatever the individual sacrifice, the key point about this card is that you make your own decision consciously to give one thing up so that you may get something you prize more highly.

NAME

PLACE

DATE

TIME

Colouring exercise
As you colour in this image, think of the various ways there are to make sacrifices. Reflect on your own experiences as well as in a broader context.

Personal association
Now consider your personal feelings about sacrifices. Think of things you have chosen to give up and how those decisions have altered your life.

What this image means in my life ⎯⎯⎯⎯⎯⎯⎯⎯⎯⎯⎯⎯⎯⎯⎯⎯⎯⎯⎯⎯⎯⎯

Readings in which it was significant ⎯⎯⎯⎯⎯⎯⎯⎯⎯⎯⎯⎯⎯⎯⎯⎯⎯⎯⎯

See Reading Record Sheet of ⎯⎯⎯⎯⎯⎯⎯⎯⎯⎯⎯⎯⎯⎯⎯⎯⎯⎯⎯⎯⎯⎯⎯

DEATH

DEATH

The Death card may cause alarm to those unfamiliar with tarot simply because of its title, so it is important to be clear that it is not about physical death but a time of death within life. In the same way that The Fool symbolizes a time of birth or new beginnings, so Death is a time for endings. Life is a constant cycle of deaths and rebirths, with each stage ending naturally when it is lived out. Each person's life changes and develops physically and psychologically, and Death marks each transition stage. The skeleton's headdress is the shroud that was once the swaddling cloth of birth; the boat on the distant river symbolizes both cradle and coffin, birth and death, which are forever inextricably linked. A bishop stands on Death's path, as does a beautiful woman and a child, while a king lies dead. This shows that Death comes to us all and that beauty, wealth or holiness offer no protection. When something has outlived its usefulness, it is time for it to die.

Within a reading

Death heralds the inevitable ending of something, yet whenever there is an end there is always a new beginning. The change and transformation this card heralds may be desired or not; whichever it is, it cannot be avoided.

Student comments

GERALDINE (62) *I have experienced Death in many ways throughout my life. Looking back, I see clearly the new horizons that lay beyond each transforming experience of death. My marriage, the birth of my daughter, the house move, the divorce – these instances all involved death and rebirth. Latterly my own business was born and the sale of that marked another death. At the moment I am in the early stages of a new study which fascinates and excites me. Reflecting on those periods in my life – some happy, some sad – I see Death standing behind them all, but not maliciously; only in a way that is natural and necessary.*

Geraldine is right to identify so many of her life's experiences – some of which have felt positive, others negative – with the card of Death. It is important to respect Death by mourning, whether the loss is related to joyful occasions like getting married or sad endings like divorce. Death reflects change, but is not specific about whether the change feels good or bad. The card itself simply marks a period of transition.

NAME

DATE

PLACE

TIME

Colouring exercise
As you colour in the
image, pay attention to
the various symbols such
as the hourglass of time,
which marks out the time
allotted for everything
on earth.

Personal association
Reflect on your own
feelings about Death and
recall your experiences
of periods of transition in
your life. When reading
for others it is important
that you can reflect on the
issues it highlights for
yourself.

What this image means in my life _____

_____

_____

_____

Readings in which it was significant _____

_____

_____

_____

See Reading Record Sheet of _____

THE DEVIL

The Devil is a strange creature – part man, part bull, part goat – symbolizing the many components of human nature, and his wings symbolize the intellect. He looks down on a naked man and woman who have taken on some of The Devil's characteristics. They have horns and tails, and chains encircle their necks; though their hands are free they choose to remain in shackles. The Devil is a symbol of repression or lack of conscious awareness. When we are unconscious we are vulnerable because we are not alert to dangers. The Devil symbolizes the dark, shadowy side of our personality we least care to acknowledge. This includes those lustful, greedy, cruel or ruthless aspects within us all, which we dislike. However, if we refuse to acknowledge them, or pretend they do not exist in us, only in others, we are vulnerable to our own destructive capabilities. If we do not have the courage for this we are doomed to live in fear and ignorance of ourselves.

THE DEVIL

Within a reading

The Devil stands for blocks and inhibitions within the psyche, which, if released, can provide positive energy. This card opens up opportunities for releasing energy, which in turn can unleash creative potential; it is up to each individual, however, to work on freeing themselves from their bondage.

Student comments

ALEX (34) *I see The Devil as an image for certain stages I have undergone in therapy, especially exploring the concept of the shadow. I have gradually been coming to terms with aspects of myself I do not like, accepting that they belong to me. As a result I feel more tolerance for both others and myself. When I get into a rage, I don't blame the world; I ask myself what is going on inside me, which ultimately helps me feel more potent and in charge of my life rather than at the mercy of my moods. I like the image of The Devil; he means hard work on an inner level but for worthwhile results.*

The Devil is indeed a potent image for self-understanding. In the card, the couple are not attempting to do anything for themselves, suggesting a lack of engagement with their own lives. Their creative power is chained, yet it could be liberated; they need not remain captive.

NAME

PLACE

DATE

TIME

Colouring exercise
As you work on this image, think about your associations with The Devil. How do you feel about him? Does he frighten or interest you? Choose colours to reflect your feelings.

Personal association
Think about how you see The Devil in your own life and work out what influence you feel he has. Are you familiar with the concept of owning your own shadow?

What this image means in my life _____

_____

_____

_____

Readings in which it was significant _____

_____

_____

_____

See Reading Record Sheet of _____

THE TOWER

The Tower shows a dramatic storm with lightning striking the top of a tall building. The flames flaring from the roof represent divine enlightenment, which burns away false values. Towers are imprisoning structures; they are narrow and restricting, and do not allow for much expansion. As the only man-made image in the tarot, The Tower represents external circumstances that repress internal development. It symbolizes the aspects of society that may curb creative impulses or inhibit growth. When something becomes too limiting it must be changed. The dramatic image of the lightning-struck Tower describes the powerful sense of understanding leading to a breakthrough. The flash of light helps us see what is truly important on an individual inner level. Three narrow windows at the top of The Tower stand for high achievement in the material world, which may not be as fulfilling as one first believes.

THE TOWER

Within a reading

The Tower stands for the need to change, sometimes drastically, old ways which have become outdated, rigid or imprisoning.

Student comments

JAMES (33) *The Tower makes me think of a very difficult phase I went through during my adolescence. My parents were very religious and forced their ideas and beliefs onto my sister and me with great conviction. My sister was fine with it all, but I didn't share any of their views. I hated their restrictive, indoctrinating beliefs, and as I grew older I refused to conform. This caused some violent arguments and eventually resulted in my breaking away from the family in a dramatic way. It was awful. I was a huge disappointment to my parents, which I do regret, as they are not 'bad' people, just different to me. I just did not want to subscribe to their views. These days we agree to differ, which is better, and I now dare to appreciate some of what they taught me. At the time, however, the only way I could set myself free was to destroy the family structure and find myself in my own way. It was painful but necessary.*

James's experience of The Tower is a good example of the kind of feelings the card may describe. There are times in most of our lives when we must stand up and be counted for who we are and what we believe. The Tower reflects such a time, when we must face ourselves honestly.

NAME

DATE

PLACE

TIME

Colouring exercise
As you colour this image, try to get in touch with the feeling of breaking down imprisoning structures to release energy. Use colours that help you reflect these feelings.

Personal association
Think of times in your life that correspond to the energy of The Tower. Consider the consequences that have followed such periods of sudden, dramatic change.

What this image means in my life _____

_____

_____

_____

Readings in which it was significant _____

_____

_____

_____

See Reading Record Sheet of _____

THE STAR

After the soul-searching that characterizes the previous cards, The Star brings some light relief. One of the most positive cards in the deck, The Star is a powerful symbol of hope. The eight-pointed star stands for rebirth and renewal. The maiden pours water freely into the Pool of Memory, which stands near the gates of the underworld in myth. We need to remember the positive to sustain us in times of difficulty, and we must remember the negative to restrain ourselves in times of joy. The butterfly is a symbol of resurrection. On the distant tree is an ibis, the bird of immortality, symbolizing the spirit's capacity to rise to the highest level of consciousness. Stars are ancient symbols of hope and guiding lights – something far away but very powerful – which the alchemists connected with the imagination.

THE STAR

Within a reading

The Star signifies optimism and the promising dawn of a new and better day. After darkness there is light; after despair there is the gift of hope which The Star promises.

Student comments

CARA (24) *The Star reminds me of how I regained hope after a bitter disappointment. A relationship that meant everything to me ended abruptly and I returned home in tears, convinced my heart would break. I felt so utterly wretched I feared that I could not survive the pain. I know this sounds a little silly now, but as I went to sleep I remember thinking that the pain was so intense I would surely die in the night. When I woke up I remember thinking, 'OK, as I didn't die in the night it means the pain is survivable so I can and will get over this.' And so I found that glimmer of hope I needed to carry on.*

The Star is an image of the hope we need when things look impossible and we fear we cannot carry on. There are times in all our lives – and Cara's story sums her experience up beautifully – when we need to find that tiny pinprick of light to lead us through the darkness. Sailors and travellers have used the stars in the night skies as guides on journeys for centuries. We still use them now as we use The Star in the tarot as an inner guide to keep us going when life seems just too hard.

NAME

DATE

PLACE

TIME

Colouring exercise
As you colour in this image, think of how you relate to the stars and what they mean for you. Choose colours to reflect your association with this image.

Personal association
Think of times in your life when you have both lost and found hope. Consider how The Star figures in your own life and in the lives of those around you.

What this image means in my life ⎯⎯⎯⎯⎯⎯⎯⎯⎯⎯⎯⎯⎯⎯⎯⎯⎯⎯⎯⎯⎯⎯⎯

Readings in which it was significant ⎯⎯⎯⎯⎯⎯⎯⎯⎯⎯⎯⎯⎯⎯⎯⎯⎯⎯⎯⎯⎯

See Reading Record Sheet of ⎯⎯⎯⎯⎯⎯⎯⎯⎯⎯⎯⎯⎯⎯⎯⎯⎯⎯⎯⎯⎯⎯⎯⎯⎯

THE MOON

The Moon is traditionally associated with deceit and illusion, partly due to the fact that the ruler of the night is inconsistent. The moon is constantly shape-shifting, from new to full to old, and every month she completes the cycle representing birth, maturity and death. This cycle corresponds to the three faces of the feminine: virgin (High Priestess, potential unfulfilled), mother (Empress, potential fulfilled) and crone (Moon, potential used up). The Moon is both womb and tomb, the place from which all life springs and to which all life eventually returns. In the foreground is the Pool of Forgetfulness, or of the unconscious mind. According to mythology, this lies next to the Pool of Memory in the underworld. Souls may drink from either pool before returning to the land of the living so they may forget or remember their underworld experience.

THE MOON

Within a reading

The Moon points to a period of uncertainty and lack of clarity. The night is not the best time to make important decisions; reason and logic need the light of day. The Moon represents a time when problems can best be understood through dreams and intuitions.

Student comments

SUSAN (51) *I like the image of The Moon better these days, as I feel less anxious when I think about the future. I used to hate the uncertainty symbolized by The Moon, and the idea of 'wait and see' drove me crazy. Nowadays I feel more comfortable with the notion that things will emerge in their own good time, so when The Moon appears in a reading I know it is a period when things will not be clear and decisions should not be made in a hurry. I have confidence in the gestation period I associate with The Moon, and understand that whatever is forming deep in the womb of the unconscious is not ready to be seen yet. I have learned it is best to wait with patience rather than try to hurry the process along.*

Susan has captured the essence of The Moon well. It symbolizes a time for allowing something to come to fruition naturally, in its own time, rather than trying to force things to happen before they are ready. The nighttime is dark so The Moon card means waiting for the dawn to break before deciding which way to go.

NAME

DATE

PLACE

TIME

Colouring exercise
Use your own choice
of colours to reflect your
feelings about The Moon.
Think about the emotions
the image evokes. Does
it scare or comfort you?

Personal association
Think about The Moon
in relation to your own
life. Compare a problem
you wake up with in the
middle of the night to one
you tackle in daylight.

What this image means in my life _____

_____

_____

_____

Readings in which it was significant _____

_____

_____

_____

See Reading Record Sheet of _____

THE SUN

THE SUN

In contrast to the eerie darkness of The Moon, The Sun appears light and fruitful. Heliotrope, oranges and sunflowers, all solar plants, appear above the laurel hedge, which is sacred to the sun god Apollo and symbolizes success and victory. Both straight and wavy rays emanate from the bright sun, symbolizing the positive, life-giving aspects of solar energy as well as the destructive rays that cause drought and death. Apollo's arrows can both cure and kill, just as the sun can ripen fruits or create deserts. The child riding the white horse represents life and new energy; his red scarf symbolizes energy and passion. The Sun and Moon were twins in mythology so they form the two halves of a whole. The Sun is masculine and represents creativity in an active way with clear perception and rationality. The Moon is feminine and represents creativity in a passive fashion; her way of operating is subtle, nebulous and uncertain. The Sun and Moon need each other equally because excessive solar energy is exhausting and can make things too hot and dry, while too much lunar energy is depressing and can make things cold and wet.

Within a reading
While The Moon suggests uncertainty and indecision, so The Sun stands for positive decisions, optimism, good cheer and success, as well as an irrepressible zest for life.

Student comments
CARA (24) *For me, The Sun is about warmth, brightness and optimism. I identify it with the kind of hope I feel in the morning when, whatever kind of a night it has been, the sun rises and heralds a new day where anything is possible. A recent example is when I was camping with friends. We were miserable because it was too cold to sleep and the night seemed endless, but the moment the first dawn rays shone through into the tent our spirits rose and we welcomed the action of a new day. The first tentative appearance of the sun was enough to make us get up, start cooking breakfast and carry on with our hike.*

Cara's associations reflect the positive action and energy typical of The Sun, which brings light in the form of understanding and ability to make things happen. The Sun is also symbolic of the artistic drives that require confidence, optimism and basic trust to complete creative projects.

NAME

DATE

PLACE

TIME

Colouring exercise
Choose colours to reflect the energy of The Sun. Think about the difference in feeling as you colour this card compared to colouring The Moon.

Personal association
Call to mind your own feelings about The Sun. Think of situations that conjure up positive feelings such as successes or victories. Note down particular instances you feel are representative of solar energy.

What this image means in my life _____

_____

_____

_____

Readings in which it was significant _____

_____

_____

_____

See Reading Record Sheet of _____

JUDGEMENT

Judgement is an image of resurrection. Three figures – a man, woman and child representing mind, body and spirit respectively – rise up from their coffins to greet the angel, a symbol of new life, of fresh opportunities and of being given another chance. We cannot see the gender of the child as it reflects the new self, still unformed and yet to be identified, existing only in potential. The red cross on the white flag forms quarters symbolizing the four elements, all opposites which meet and merge at the central point. The coffins float on the ocean, which represents the waters of the womb, thus symbolizing the crucial moment between life and death, and death and rebirth. Judgement suggests a summing-up of events, a time to balance accounts and an opportunity to assess and evaluate one's progress to date.

JUDGEMENT

Within a reading

Judgement represents a time for personal evaluation and learning lessons gained through experience. It is a time to reap the rewards, or otherwise, for past efforts.

Student comments

JAMES (33) *I associate Judgement with the way I felt when I learned my final school exam results were poor. This was partly due to the subject choices I had made, and partly because I hadn't done enough work. Whatever the reasons, I had to face the fact that the results were due to my own actions. So I decided to make some different choices. I abandoned the idea of studying medicine, retook some exams at night school and applied to study law, which was something I wanted to do. I think of the Judgement card in this context because I knew I had to accept responsibility for the position I found myself in. It was no good blaming anyone else; it was up to me to sow the next set of seeds for the future, and I was determined to do it differently.*

Judgement is about 'sowing what you reap', as James rightly points out. Once that notion is understood, it is easier to make decisions for the future based on past experience. If something has been successful in the past, it makes sense to repeat it; but if not, it is wise to try something else. Although this may seem obvious, it is surprising how often we make the same mistakes. Judgement reminds us that the key to choice is to become more conscious.

NAME

DATE

PLACE

TIME

Colouring exercise
As you work on this image, think about the notion of fresh starts based on past experience. Allow yourself to embark on a short self-appraisal, being as honest as you can with yourself.

Personal association
Think of situations in your own life you can associate with Judgement. Use the student comments as a springboard for personal thought and for discussing the ideas with others.

What this image means in my life _____

_____

_____

_____

Readings in which it was significant _____

_____

_____

See Reading Record Sheet of _____

THE WORLD

The World is the final card in the Major Arcana cycle, and as such represents completion. The imagery shows a veiled figure, which may be a hermaphrodite, as an image of unification. The figure is within a laurel wreath of success, and wearing a gold crown to represent the attainment of a goal. In each corner, winged creatures represent the four seasons, the four fixed signs of the zodiac and the four elements, which the alchemists sought to blend into a perfect fifth. Success is achieved at the end of the journey because the end must always be followed by a beginning. The dancing figure of The World will soon become the baby in the womb, waiting rebirth again in the figure of The Fool. And so the cycle will start again, always the same and always different.

THE WORLD

Within a reading

The World represents a completion of a stage or phase in life. It can be seen as the achievement or realization of a particular prize or goal, and as such brings a deserved sense of triumph and exhilaration.

Student comments

CARA (24) *I associate The World with exam success. When I passed my A levels with good grades, I felt a tremendous sense of achievement. All my hard work and worry turned to relief and joy, and it was a truly fantastic moment. However, it was not long before the peak of excitement turned into a new beginning when I started at university and found myself at the bottom of the ladder again. After three years, the cycle repeated with final exams and getting my degree, culminating in another level of achievement and delight, which seemed even more important. The next step was trying to find a decent job, which has finally happened recently, so right now I am at the beginning of the next journey, back to being The Fool.*

Cara has given some literal examples of how The World card can be experienced. It can, of course, be realized in many different ways, depending on each individual's life, dreams and aspirations. Whatever a person strives to achieve, once they have achieved it they will move on to pursue the next level. This is the never-ending story of endings and new beginnings the tarot images reflect so beautifully.

NAME

PLACE

DATE

TIME

Colouring exercise
As you colour this image, concentrate on how it feels to be working on the last image in the series. If you have followed the sequence through in succession, The World card will mark your completion of a cycle.

Personal association
Think of situations you can personally associate with The World card. Note down your own experiences of endings and beginnings.

What this image means in my life ⎯⎯⎯⎯⎯⎯⎯⎯⎯⎯⎯⎯⎯⎯⎯⎯⎯⎯

Readings in which it was significant ⎯⎯⎯⎯⎯⎯⎯⎯⎯⎯⎯⎯⎯⎯⎯⎯

See Reading Record Sheet of ⎯⎯⎯⎯⎯⎯⎯⎯⎯⎯⎯⎯⎯⎯⎯⎯⎯⎯

CREATIVE INTERPRETATION

Now we have been through the seventy-eight images of the tarot deck, it is time to start using them in creative ways.

So far we have looked at the personal experiences and associations of the students in the work group. Now we will share in their spontaneous story-telling as another way of enriching and deepening your understanding of the tarot images.

In one group session we decided to play with the notion of making up a story using images chosen at random. The students each chose three cards to represent the beginning, middle and end of a story. The group was told to use the cards as a springboard for making up an instant story, drawing upon ideas and information gained in earlier sessions as well as using the image itself as inspiration.

CARA DREW:
Queen of Swords, Ace of Wands and Seven of Pentacles. She called her story:
'The Woman who Learned to Love Gardens'.

QUEEN OF SWORDS: *Once upon a time there was a woman who was beautiful and clever, but disappointed in love. Her relationships had been difficult, and none of her lovers had managed to please her because she always expected too much of them. She finally gave up trying to find happiness in relationships and decided to spend her time alone, reading and listening to music, but she felt lonely and sad.*

ACE OF WANDS: *One day, quite by chance, she was given a book on gardening and started to get quite interested in the prospect of redesigning her roof terrace. This was a completely new area for her, as she did not usually like the idea of physical work. She suddenly, and quite uncharacteristically, found herself getting excited about plants in pots and trelliswork with climbing roses.*

SEVEN OF PENTACLES: *The woman started to work on her roof garden. She first made some careful plans on paper, and read lots of books. However, you cannot create a garden, even a little one, without getting your hands dirty, and when she started to plant out her flowers something changed in her. She found the practical work immensely satisfying. When she had finished her little roof terrace she decided to sell her flat and buy a house with a bigger garden so she could have a new challenge.*

Juliet's comments
As Cara chose the three cards randomly, she spontaneously came up with the above story. She did not limit her associations to the pictorial images on the cards; she also used her knowledge of their divinatory meanings. She first drew on her understanding of the Queen of Swords as one who has suffered in the area of relationships and now mistrusts them because they so often fail to meet expectations. Cara remembered that the Queen of Swords is an air card, and one of the qualities of this element is an expectation

of perfection that does not translate easily into human life and relationships. In her story, she therefore had her 'heroine' give up on relationships and retreat into intellectual pursuits, typical of the air element.

Cara then used the fiery, creative Ace of Wands to inspire her heroine and draw her out of herself to do something completely out of character. The Ace of Wands is a card of inspiration and ideas, and because Cara noticed the last card was the Seven of Pentacles, she decided that the Ace of Wands' inspiration would be of an earthy nature, in keeping with the suit of Pentacles. The Seven of Pentacles signifies that something is accomplished while a new challenge is ready to be faced if chosen. With this in mind, Cara decided to have her heroine inspired to create a roof terrace – a nice earthy image – with her next challenge being to create an even larger, more complex garden.

As you can see, the idea is not to try to create a bestselling story, but to work with the random images in an impromptu way. You do not necessarily need to come up with a plausible story, or even a particularly exciting one. It is enough just to give your imagination plenty of scope and associate to the images freely.

GERALDINE DREW:

Eight of Wands, Ten of Wands and Five of Cups. She called her story: *The Man who Learned that Work was not Everything'*.

EIGHT OF WANDS: *There was once a young man who had many great ideas. He had a good imagina-tion and wonderfully original notions. One day he started to put some of his visions into action. For a while, everything he dreamed of seemed to work out beautifully. His ideas for businesses and creative ventures all seemed to grow and flourish. He was happy and energetic, full of enthusiasm and optimism.*

TEN OF WANDS: *Alas, although everything around him seemed to be growing at a fast pace, the man could not keep up. He wasn't very good at saying 'no', so every time he thought of something new he acted on it. He was offered many interesting busi-ness and creative opportunities, and he accepted everything. Eventually he found himself over-stretched and burdened. After a while, the things that used to excite him started to worry him, and although he had become very successful he did not feel that way inside. He felt stressed and over-wrought but still he didn't say 'no'. He refused to turn anything away and he kept on struggling with his heavy load.*

FIVE OF CUPS: *The man had become so concerned with his business projects and creative endeavours that he had been neglecting his wife and family for a long time. He had not stopped loving them at all, but he didn't have enough time for them, nor did he make the time. One evening he arrived home from work late as usual and found they had gone. His wife had finally had enough and wanted a divorce. The man was heartbroken. He realized what he had lost and deeply regretted his obsession with work but it was too late. For the first time in years he allowed himself to have feelings about what he was doing with his life, and as he read the sad note his wife had written he cried bitter tears of regret. He caught sight of a photograph on the wall of his whole family together and wondered if perhaps there might be a way he could still put things right.*

Juliet's comments

Geraldine's story keeps close to the meanings of the three random cards. The Eight of Wands represents a time of great excitement and action, while the Ten of Wands reflects a burden. A key point, which Geraldine manages to capture in her story, is the sense of a lack of boundary that is often a feature in the suit of Wands. The energy of fire means that reality and earthy limits are seen as boring and therefore ignored, and whenever a function is ignored it creates trouble. A good analogy for that is the story of Sleeping Beauty, where the 'bad fairy' is left off the guest list and ends up creating a great deal of trouble as a result. Things do not go away just because they are ignored, as Geraldine's 'hero' finds out to his cost. Geraldine decides that her hero should wake up to the imbalances in his life by losing something on a feeling level. The Five of Cups suggests disappointment, regret, sorrow or the loss of a loving relationship, yet at the end of her story Geraldine manages to bring in the notion that perhaps – as hinted at by the two upright cups in the image – all is not necessarily lost.

Try this Yourself

This form of instant story creation can be great fun if you let your imagination run loose while staying within the structure of what you know about the cards. Why not look at both sets of the above three cards and see how many different scenarios you can come up with? Alternatively, you could draw three cards yourself and associate to them spontaneously to see where your imagination takes you.

This technique is not the same as free association, which works in a different way. Free association involves reacting to the card images without knowing anything about the card's meanings. It can be fun to experiment with friends who know nothing of the meanings to see what sort of instant, uninformed responses they come up with.

These exercises offer ways of stretching and stimulating the imagination and intuition. They avoid any kind of 'right or wrong' approach, which does not work well when interpreting the tarot.

RECORD SHEETS

When it comes to reading the tarot for others, the only way to learn is to experiment and practise. In the *Beginner's Guide to Tarot*, I gave many examples of different readings. However, reading a recipe is not the same as cooking the dish, so rather than give you even more examples I recommend that you do as many readings, make up as many stories (*as shown in 'Creative Interpretation', page 166*), colour in as many images, and come up with as many associations to each card as you possibly can. These are all good ways to become a sensitive and proficient tarot reader.

I have provided a number of blank spread layouts here for you to copy. You can use them to record each reading you do, whether it is for yourself or for others. By keeping a dated record and notes of each reading, you can observe over time how the cards match events as they unfold. In this way, you will gradually get a real sense of how the rhythm of life is mirrored in the tarot images.

THE CELTIC CROSS SPREAD

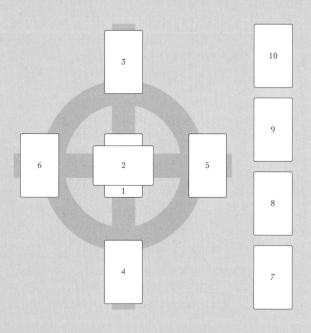

NAME _____

DATE OF READING _____

QUESTION _____

_____

_____

_____

_____

MAIN POINTS RAISED _____

_____

_____

_____

_____

_____

_____

_____

_____

_____

_____

_____

The Celtic Cross is the most well-known and widely used spread. The whole deck can be used or just the Minor Arcana if preferred. Shuffle the deck and spread the cards out face down. Select ten cards unseen from the deck and lay them out in the order below, placing the first card chosen in the first position and so on. Fill in the record so you can refer back to the reading at any time.

1 The present
2 What crosses you
3 What is above you
4 What is beneath you
5 What is behind you
6 What is before you
7 Your future position
8 How others experience you
9 Hopes and fears
10 The outcome

CARDS IN POSITION

1 _____	6 _____
2 _____	7 _____
3 _____	8 _____
4 _____	9 _____
5 _____	10 _____

THE STAR SPREAD

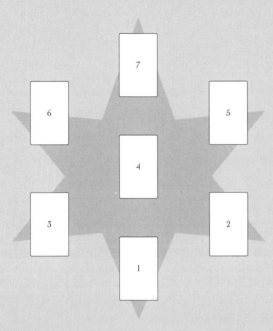

NAME

DATE OF READING

QUESTION

MAIN POINTS RAISED

This spread is particularly good for looking at spiritual or psychological issues. I recommend using the Major Arcana on its own for this reading. Separate the twenty-two Major Arcana cards, then shuffle and choose seven cards in the usual way.

1 The root of the matter or the present
2 Matters concerning heart and relationships
3 Matters concerning mind and career
4 Heart of the matter
5 Unconscious desires
6 Conscious desires
7 Top of the matter or conclusion

CARDS IN POSITION

1 _____   5 _____

2 _____   6 _____

3 _____   7 _____

4 _____

THE HORSESHOE SPREAD

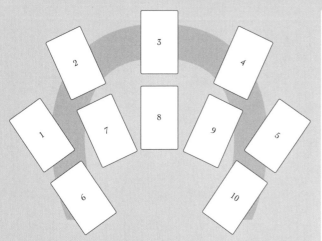

NAME
_____

DATE OF READING
_____

QUESTION
_____
_____
_____
_____

MAIN POINTS RAISED
_____
_____
_____
_____
_____
_____
_____
_____
_____

This spread can use only five cards or be expanded to ten cards if preferred. You can put two cards in each position to give you more information and a fuller picture. Choose the cards in the usual way, shuffling and selecting from the unseen deck. This spread is suitable for use with the whole deck.

1 (6) Present position
2 (7) What you presently expect
3 (8) What you do not expect
4 (9) Short-term future
5 (10) Long-term future

CARDS IN POSITION

1 _____	6 _____
2 _____	7 _____
3 _____	8 _____
4 _____	9 _____
5 _____	10 _____

THE PLANETARY SPREAD

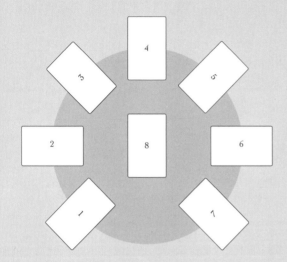

NAME

DATE OF READING

QUESTION

_____

_____

_____

_____

MAIN POINTS RAISED

_____

_____

_____

_____

_____

_____

_____

_____

_____

_____

_____

_____

_____

Choose eight cards for this spread from the whole deck, shuffling and selecting as before. This is a good spread for those familiar with astrology, as the meaning of the cards can be seen through the lens of seven ancient planets, with the eighth position representing the outcome of the reading.

1 The Moon (home and family life)
2 The Sun (achievement, reward)
3 Mercury (mental ability, work and career)
4 Venus (relationships and love life)
5 Mars (quarrels or conflicts)
6 Jupiter (gain, growth, expansion)
7 Saturn (restriction, limitation, inhibition)
8 The outcome (conclusion)

CARDS IN POSITION

1 _____   5 _____

2 _____   6 _____

3 _____   7 _____

4 _____   8 _____

THE COMPASS SPREAD

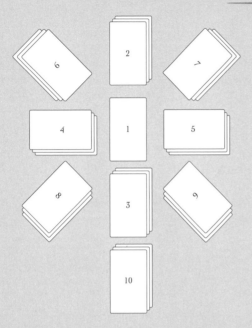

NAME _____

DATE OF READING _____

QUESTION _____

_____

_____

_____

MAIN POINTS RAISED

_____

_____

_____

_____

_____

_____

_____

_____

_____

_____

_____

_____

When your confidence builds, try this twenty-eight-card spread. Shuffle the whole deck, choose one card and place it face down. This represents you in the present. Then choose three cards and place them in a pile in the North position, and continue placing piles of three cards round the points of the compass in the order shown. Take each pile in turn and read the three cards together. Finally, combine all twenty-eight cards into a coherent reading.

1 Central Position (where you are in life)
2 North (general atmosphere surrounding you and the question asked of the reading)
3 South (matters which are within your control)
4 West (past issues)
5 East (future issues)
6 North-west (house and home)
7 North-east (hopes and fears)
8 South-west (what you don't expect)
9 South-east (what you do expect)
10 Below South (what is sure to come)

CARDS IN POSITION

1 _____   6 _____

2 _____   7 _____

3 _____   8 _____

4 _____   9 _____

5 _____   10 _____

The Horoscope Spread

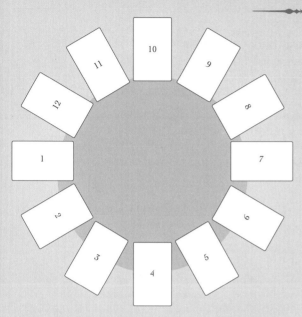

NAME _____

DATE OF READING _____

QUESTION _____

_____

_____

_____

MAIN POINTS RAISED

_____

_____

_____

_____

_____

_____

_____

_____

_____

_____

_____

This spread can be read in two ways. The first is as a Yearly Forecast, to give you an indication of the year ahead. Starting at the nine o'clock position, deal out twelve cards anticlockwise. Card 1 represents the current month. A thirteenth card can be placed at the centre as a general indicator for the year.

Alternatively, this spread can be interpreted in terms of the twelve houses into which a horoscope is divided, with Card 1 marking the first house:

1 Yourself or the one you are reading for
2 Money and possessions
3 Mental capacities, self-expression, siblings
4 Childhood environment, home life
5 Love life, pleasures, romance, children
6 Health and work
7 Marriage/emotional or business relationships
8 Endings and new beginnings
9 Philosophical views, dreams, higher education
10 Career, status, reputation
11 Friends and social life, hopes and ambitions
12 The secret/unknown, the unconscious mind

CARDS IN POSITION

1 _____	7 _____
2 _____	8 _____
3 _____	9 _____
4 _____	10 _____
5 _____	11 _____
6 _____	12 _____

FURTHER READING AND RESOURCES

Beginner's Guide to Tarot, Juliet Sharman-Burke, Connections 2001
Jung and Tarot: An Archetypal Journey, Sallie Nichols, Red Wheel/Weiser, 2000
Mastering the Tarot, Juliet Sharman-Burke, Connections 2000
The Mythic Tarot, Juliet Sharman-Burke and Liz Greene, Rider, 1986
The Tarot Handbook, Hajo Banzhaf, US Games, 2003
The Tarot: History, Mystery and Lore, Cynthia Giles, Fireside, 1994
Tarot and the Journey of the Hero, Hajo Banzhaf, Red Wheel/Weiser, 2000
Tarot Mirrors: Reflections of Personal Meaning, Mary K. Greer, Newcastle Publishing Co., 1988
Tarot Symbolism, Robert V. O'Neill, Fairway Press, 1994
Understanding the Tarot, Juliet Sharman-Burke, Rider, 1998

Useful Websites

www.tabi.org.uk
www.tarot.com
www.tarothermit.com/infosheet.htm
Sources of the Waite/Smith Tarot Symbols
www.geocities.com/~ninalee//oneill/

For Tarot and Astrology Courses contact:

The Centre for Psychological Astrology
BCM Box 1815
London
WC1N 3XX
www.cpalondon.com

ACKNOWLEDGEMENTS

I would like to take this opportunity of sincerely thanking Alex, Cara, Geraldine, James and Susan for generously allowing me to use their personal thoughts, feelings and associations to the cards which they shared during our work together. We all learned so much from each other and I hope that readers of this book might consider following their example, and setting up similar work/discussion groups to enrich their own studies.

I would also like to thank Ian and Nick and all those at Eddison Sadd for their continued support and enthusiasm for my work and for their help with this book. My thanks also to my agent Barbara Levy who has been so good to me for so many years, and to my family who got used to going without dinner while I wrote this!

EDDISON • SADD EDITIONS

Editorial Director Ian Jackson
Managing Editor Tessa Monina
Copy-editor Michele Turney
Proofreader Nikky Twyman
Art Director Elaine Partington
Mac Designer Brazzle Atkins
Production Sarah Rooney and Nick Eddison